On Politics and Policy

On Politics and Policy

◆

Views on Freedom from an American Conservative

A project of Frontiers of Freedom Institute

The Best of George C. Landrith

iUniverse, Inc.
New York Lincoln Shanghai

On Politics and Policy
Views on Freedom from an American Conservative

iUniverse, Inc.

For information address:
iUniverse, Inc.
2021 Pine Lake Road, Suite 100
Lincoln, NE 68512
www.iuniverse.com

ISBN: 0-595-33571-3

Printed in the United States of America

For my wife, Laura, and our seven children
—Carl, David, Jenae, Rachel, Thomas, Jefferson and CJ—
who have patiently and graciously tolerated my
preoccupation with politics and policy.

And for Ronald Wilson Reagan, whose leadership, vision
and courage changed America and the world—making
them freer, safer, and more prosperous.

Contents

Introduction

When I tell people what I do for living, one question is almost inevitable—"What's a think-tank?" here's my answer: Think tanks analyze and discuss policy and political matters, but don't get involved in endorsing the candidates who are often tied to issues. To the casual observer this may be a fine line, but the difference is important. One cannot divorce politicians from the discussion of public policy issues. But one can discuss these issues without calling for the election or defeat of candidates. I have always been happy to look at the issues and the personalities behind the issues. Often I praise or criticize politicians for the positions that they take on the issues. But that is not the same thing as endorsing candidates. I prefer to endorse ideas, not personalities.

I suppose this book could be described as a "best of" collection—a compilation of articles I've written in recent years. Each article has its own beginning and ending, but is not necessarily dependent on previous or subsequent articles. My purpose in writing this book is to provide a guide or handbook to many of the most pressing public policy issues of our time. Representative democracy works best when the citizenry is well educated and knowledgeable on the issues.

Unlike the mainstream media who disingenuously claim to be unbiased, I freely admit my biases. I think the reader should know where I stand. So here goes.

I believe America is the greatest nation on earth. I believe the hand of divine Providence guided great men like George Washington, John Adams, Thomas Jefferson, Benjamin Franklin and many others to establish a nation dedicated to the proposition "that all men are created equal, that they are endowed by their Creator with certain unalienable Rights, that among these are Life, Liberty and the pursuit of Happiness." While I understand that America is not perfect, I believe that no nation has done more to protect and expand freedom. No nation has been a truer friend to freedom than America.

I believe in free markets as opposed to government command and control systems. Free markets decentralize power into the hands of millions of workers, consumers and business owners. Government run command and control systems concentrate power into the hands of a few politicians or bureaucrats. While some basic regulations can benefit the marketplace, too many regulatory schemes are counterproductive and needlessly burdensome. A free market system is most likely to promote individual liberty and create prosperity.

I also believe that liberty is under assault in America—from within and from without. America has enemies throughout the world. The events of September 11, 2001 prove this axiomatically. As the nation that most embodies the precepts of freedom, America draws the hatred of those who loathe liberty. America's freedom also has enemies from within. There are Americans who pay lip service to our Founders and the principles of our founding documents, but essentially view the constitutional system they created as an impediment to "good government." These people, often unwittingly, put America's freedom at risk in the long run.

I am a proud and optimistic conservative in the tradition of one of our nation's greatest presidents—Ronald Reagan. He was a skilled leader and he led America in the right direction—making America and the world safer, freer and more prosperous. Like President Reagan, I believe America's best days lay ahead and that every American must his part to make it so.

Below is a list of ten of my specific beliefs (or biases).

I believe…

- The most basic moral obligation of the federal government is to defend America, which requires military and economic preparation and strength.

- Property rights and economic freedom are the fertile soil in which all other rights grow and thrive.

- The Constitution's enumerated and limited powers, checks and balances, federalism, separation of powers, and guarantee of basic rights are the foundation of America's freedom.

- Life, Liberty, and the pursuit of Happiness and each of the rights guaranteed in the Constitution are necessary to the foundation of freedom—including the right to bear arms and to not be deprived of property without just compensation.

- The courts have a constitutional duty to faithfully and strictly interpret the law and the Constitution and may not invent or create new law.

- Justice is the equal treatment of all *individuals* regardless of ethnicity or religion. Fabricating *group* rights undermines individual freedom and civil rights.

- Taxes may be legitimately imposed *only* to the extent necessary to pay for the essential and constitutionally permitted activities of government.

- Government mandates and regulations too often exceed constitutional authority, waste resources, erode freedom, diminish property rights, and produce harmful unintended consequences.

- To remove sound science from public policy is legislative and regulatory malpractice. To employ junk science in public policy is unethical and irresponsible.

- Basic standards of morality and civic virtue are essential to maintaining America's economic strength, military might, and freedom.

Well, now I've disclosed my beliefs and biases. You've been warned. Read at your own peril!

1

Elections & Politics

John Kerry vs. John Kerry

(Originally published in August 2004)

John Kerry claims he has been a strong, consistent voice for America's security and safety. But saying it doesn't make it so. Kerry started off supporting the war. Then in a political move, he decided to oppose the war. Now, he's apparently returned to lukewarm support of the war. That is not consistent, decisive leadership. But don't take my word for it. Read Kerry's own words.

On September 23, 2001, on CBS's *Face the Nation*, Kerry said, "[I]t is something that we know, for instance, Saddam Hussein has used weapons of mass destruction against his own people, and there is some evidence of their efforts to try to secure these kinds of weapons and even test them."

On December 11, 2001 on Fox News' *The O'Reilly Factor*, Kerry said, "[Saddam] is and has acted like a terrorist…[I] think we ought to put the heat on Saddam Hussein…no matter what the evidence is about September 11th…"

Three days later, on CNN's *Larry King Live*, Kerry said, "I think we clearly have to keep the pressure on terrorism globally. This doesn't end with Afghanistan by any imagination…Terrorism is a global menace. It's a scourge. And it is absolutely vital that we continue, for instance, against Saddam Hussein."

On September 6, 2002, Kerry wrote in *The New York Times*, "If Saddam Hussein is unwilling to bend to the international community's already existing order, then he will have invited enforcement…even if that enforcement is mostly at the hands of the United States, a right we retain even if the Security Council fails to act."

On September 17, 2002 on MSNBC's *Hardball*, Kerry said, "But the president, as I also wrote in that article, always reserves the right to act unilaterally to protect the interests of our country."

On October 11, 2002, Kerry voted for the Iraq War Resolution.

But then the Democratic nomination picked-up steam and Howard Dean rode his anti-war rhetoric to an early and impressive lead. After seeing Dean's success, Kerry began his migration and another of his famous flip-flops was set in motion.

On May 3, 2003, at the Democratic candidate's debate, ABC News moderator George Stephanopoulos asked Howard Dean, "Now, you've criticized Senator Kerry on the campaign trail saying he's tried to have it both ways on the issue of Iraq. Was that answer clear enough for you?" Howard Dean didn't really answer. But Senator Joe Lieberman critiqued Dean and Kerry, "[B]oth have sent an uncertain message, one in principled opposition to the war, Governor Dean. The other an ambivalence about the war, which does not, will not, give the people confidence about our party's willingness to make the tough decisions to protect their security in a world after September 11th."

On September 14, 2003, on CBS's *Face the Nation*, when asked about voting on the $87 billion to fund the troops, Kerry said, "I don't think any Senator is going to abandon our troops and recklessly leave Iraq to whatever follows as a result of simply cutting and running. That's irresponsible...I don't think anyone in the Congress is going to not give our troops ammunition, not give our troops the ability...to defend themselves. We're not going to cut and run..."

One month later, on October 17, 2003, Senator Kerry voted NO on $87 billion for our troops in Afghanistan and Iraq—a vote Kerry previously called "irresponsible," "cutting and running" and "abandoning our troops."

On January 6, 2004, on MSNBC's *Hardball*, Chris Matthews asked Kerry, "Are you one of the anti-war candidates?" Kerry responded, "I am. Yeah."

On March 16, 2004, Kerry explained his flip-flop with these fateful words, "I actually did vote for the $87 billion, before I voted against it..."

On July 21, 2004, CBS's Dan Rather asked Kerry about the apparent contradiction of his votes saying, "Voted for the war, but now didn't vote for the money to finance the war." Kerry responded defensively, "That's not a flip-flop. That's not a flip-flop."

On August 9, 2004, John Kerry switched directions again and said he would have voted for the resolution authorizing force against Iraq even had he known that no weapons of mass destruction would be found.

Again in August, Kerry said, "I will have significant, enormous reduction in the level of troops."

John Kerry can say he hasn't flip-flopped, but saying it doesn't make it so. Call me old fashioned, but I'd like a commander-in-chief who can make up his mind—especially when the safety of the nation is at stake.

Endangering the Economy & National Security

(Originally published in April 2004)

Democratic presidential candidate John Kerry says that he will do a better job building a strong economy and protecting America from terrorist threats. Kerry criticizes President George W. Bush for not agreeing to the Global Warming Treaty (also known as the Kyoto Protocol) or at least not supporting the McCain-Lieberman bill, which would implement the Protocol's restrictive energy rationing approach. Incredibly, Kerry argues that France and Germany would have been more helpful in the war in Iraq if only Bush were more support- ive of the Kyoto Protocol.

This, of course, ignores that France and other nations had under-the-table deals with Iraq. Regardless of Bush's stance on the Kyoto Treaty, France and oth- ers profiting illegally from Iraq's oil would never have supported the United States in Iraq.

Kerry's approach is odd because the Kyoto Protocol and its legislative cousin, the McCain-Lieberman bill, would harm both the economy and our national security. On the economic front, Kyoto and McCain-Lieberman would dramati- cally increase fuel and energy costs. They would additionally kill jobs in virtually every sector—but transportation and manufacturing would be particularly hard hit. Thus, it seems odd to hear Kerry criticize Bush for not doing enough to strengthen the economy while Kerry simultaneously supports Kyoto and McCain-Lieberman which would hammer the economy, kill job growth and drive energy prices through the roof.

As odd as it is for a man claiming to be committed to strengthening the econ- omy to support Kyoto and McCain-Lieberman, it is even more odd to claim to be an effective leader who will aggressively defend America while supporting such proposals.

The Kyoto Protocol would explicitly place our nation's security at risk. The treaty would require the United States to slash its carbon dioxide emissions by about 40% beginning in 2010. This would mean cutbacks in training missions, less support for deployments and continued strains on a military force that was dramatically cut during the Clinton years and stretched during the war on terror.

Unfortunately, there is no national security exception to the treaty. The treaty reads: "Emissions resulting from multi-national operations, pursuant to the UN charter, shall not be included in national totals." The treaty goes on to say,

"Emissions related to other operations shall be included in the national emissions total of one or more of the parties involved."

Here's the plain English translation: Under the treaty, America's military could not conduct training exercises unless the UN approves. Additionally, America could not take military action to defend itself unless two conditions are met: first, the UN must approve; and second, the military action must be carried out by a UN multinational force. What does this mean on a practical level?

First, training for our fighting men and women would be dramatically reduced. We would determine the level training based on how much carbon dioxide would be emitted—not how much training is needed to defend the nation or protect the lives of our troops. Cuts in training would only endanger the lives of our troops and diminish our nation's security.

Second, we would require the military to purchase equipment based on its carbon dioxide emissions, rather than effectiveness. We must provide our soldiers with the best possible equipment. Decisions about which fighter jets, bombers, tanks, missiles or helicopters to use should NOT be based on their carbon dioxide emissions, but on their ability to get the job done and protect our troops.

Third, what would happen if the United States must defend itself or protect its vital security interests and the UN refused to give its approval of the action? After the actions of France and Germany, it takes little imagination to foresee such a problem. But unless France agreed, our ability to defend ourselves would be hamstrung by the treaty's emissions requirements. We ought not enter into absurd treaties that we fear we might be forced to violate just to defend ourselves.

Any military leader worth his salt will tell you that his focus is on protecting our national security and the safety and well-being of his troops. Can you imagine telling an officer to reduce the number of bombing missions, use a smaller force or risk lives simply to appease arbitrary carbon dioxide emissions standards? Our freedom and the lives of our service men and women are much too precious for that.

Kerry says that if the Bush Administration had been more supportive of the Kyoto Protocol, France and Germany would not have blocked UN support for the war in Iraq. Aside from being totally absurd, it is troubling that Kerry believes we should adopt policies that would empower other nations to determine when we could defend ourselves. Kerry has promised to be strong on defense and to keep America safe. If his support for Kyoto is any indication, Kerry cannot be trusted to keep that promise.

It is time for America to put first things first. Freedom is the very reason this nation was founded. For more than 225 years, Americans have defended that freedom with their blood and lives. It would dishonor their heroic sacrifices and endanger our children's future to place an international emissions treaty above our ability to preserve our freedom and protect our national interests.

Happy with High Gas Prices

(Originally published in June 2004)

With higher gasoline prices at the pump, John Kerry is in full campaign mode—saying just about anything he thinks will help him win a vote, no mater how implausible. This time he promised that if elected, he would fight for lower gas prices at the pump. This is interesting because Kerry should be happy with current high fuel prices given his consistent support for higher gasoline taxes and other regulatory policies that make energy more expensive.

As a presidential candidate, Kerry promises he will be "a president who is fighting for the American worker...at the fuel pumps, to lower the price of gas." Kerry also says, "I'm going to stand up for...middle class families and all those who need relief at the pump." That is what Kerry, the presidential candidate, says now.

Yet, throughout John Kerry's long political career, he has supported increased gasoline and fuel taxes a dozen times. There is no record of Kerry having fought for lower prices at the pump.

Kerry's response to these facts is to deny "proposing" the additional taxes. Nice try, Senator Kerry, but one can *support* a new tax without *proposing* it. One can also *support* a tax increase without *voting* for it because the bill may never receive an official vote, notwithstanding one's support for the measure.

John Kerry can play childish word games all he likes, but the fact is Kerry supported a fifty-cent tax on each gallon of gasoline in 1994. Now that Kerry is running for president, he is promising to make prices lower at the pump. Kerry also twice voted for the Clinton-Gore BTU tax that would have added 7.5 cents to each gallon of gas. Eleven times, Senator Kerry voted for higher gasoline taxes. Now that he is running for president, he denies his past and promises he will work to lower gas prices.

But it does not stop there. Kerry has consistently supported energy policies that dramatically increase costs. Take for instance the energy-capping legislation named "McCain-Lieberman." John Kerry is a big supporter of this measure as well as its "cousin," the Kyoto Protocol. In a recent study conducted by Charles Rivers Associates for the United for Jobs coalition, this energy-caping, fuel-reducing, gas price-hiking legislation will do exactly the opposite of what Mr. Kerry is promising on the campaign trail. An estimated 600,000 American jobs will be lost if this legislation is passed. Families will lose an additional $2,300 in disposable income by 2020 and gas prices will zoom upward an *additional* $0.30 to $0.50 per gallon.

But now that John Kerry is running for president, he promises America that he will fight for lower gasoline prices. In his over twenty years in the U.S. Senate, he has worked for higher gas prices, but now we are to believe that as president, he would work to lower them.

Which Kerry should we believe? The senator who consistently voted to raise gasoline prices or the presidential candidate who promises to lower prices at the pump?

This is a theme with Senator Kerry. He actively supports laws that make it harder and more expensive for Americans to drive minivans, SUVs and small trucks, while he and his wife drive SUVs. But the hypocrisy does not end there. When Kerry speaks to extreme environmentalists, he touts his efforts to limit and effectively ban minivans and SUVs. But when he speaks to union workers in Detroit, Kerry brags about how he and his family proudly drive SUVs.

Which Kerry should we believe? The one who says Americans should be able to choose the automobile that meets their needs or the one who brags about trying to limit consumer choices and make larger family vehicles even more expensive?

When confronted with the inconsistent and conflicting messages to different audiences, Kerry explains that technically his wife owns the SUVs. This silly response shouldn't make anyone feel better about Kerry's duplicity and hypocrisy.

President George W. Bush has proposed a sweeping energy policy that focuses on both conservation and increased production of reliable domestic energy. Senator Kerry helped block passage of the president's energy plan. Yet, Kerry criticizes Bush for not having a plan.

This is the political world of John Kerry. Support higher gasoline taxes and claim to be for lower prices at the pump. Drive SUVs and support laws that make it more difficult and more expensive for others to do the same. Tell extreme environmentalists you've worked to limit SUVs and minivans and tell union employees you proudly drive SUVs. Obstruct the passage of the administration's workable national energy policy and criticize the president because the blocked policy is not in place.

There is something troubling about a politician spending his entire career promoting higher gasoline taxes and then, when running for president, telling folks that he will work for lower prices at the pump.

Some politicians will say anything in hopes of getting elected. As voters, it is our job to determine if the politician is speaking the truth.

Doubletalk on Jobs

(Originally published in May 2004)

Everyone understands that jobs are good for the economy. Perhaps this explains why Senator John Kerry has spent so much time painting a bleak economic picture and criticizing President George W. Bush. If Kerry can make the case that Bush's policies have killed jobs and hurt the economy, then he would have a powerful campaign tool indeed.

John Kerry and his surrogates have been trying to blame President Bush for the economic slow down and job losses that occurred after the September 11th terrorist attacks. Furthermore, Kerry promises that if elected, he will insure that the economy grows and the jobs are abundant. However, there are at least two problems with Kerry's campaign on jobs and the economy.

First, Kerry is standing in the bright sunlight but telling America that it is pouring rain. The truth is the economy is growing at a healthy and robust rate. In turn, the strong economy has encouraged a new wave of hiring. The fact is President Bush's tax cuts have helped fuel this new economic expansion and job growth. Notwithstanding the good news, Kerry is still telling Americans it is raining.

Many months before Bush ever took office, the economy slipped into a recession. Yet, Kerry blames Bush for a recession that started when Clinton and Gore were at the helm. Immediately upon taking office, Bush pushed for and got tax cuts to spur the economy. Only months later, terrorists struck America with a devastating attack that horrified America and slammed the economy. President Bush again pushed hard for tax cuts to spur the economy and give Americans more of their own money to spend on their priorities. Bush got his tax cut and the economy began to rebound. Today the economy is expanding so well that some say it is too strong and growing too fast. Some folks are never happy.

John Kerry can complain about jobs and the economy all he likes, but there is little room to complain. He truly is standing in the warm sunshine while complaining of imagined cold rain.

The second problem with Kerry's promises that he'll do a better job with the economy and jobs is that his voting record in the Senate makes it clear that jobs have *never* been his priority. In a comprehensive study of Senate voting records by the respected and nonpartisan *National Journal*, John Kerry was found to be *the most liberal senator.* That is quite an accomplishment! It takes considerable effort to make Ted Kennedy the "conservative" senator from Massachusetts.

You might ask what difference does it make whether Kerry is ultra-liberal? The answer lies in how he won the title of most liberal. To win that "prize," Kerry had to support a lot of job-killing tax increases and oppose a lot of tax cuts. Kerry voted for higher taxes and against tax cuts more than 100 times. That is a lot of taxes. He had to support a lot of job-crushing regulatory regimes. He had to consistently side with trial lawyers and fight against needed legal and regulatory reform. He had to consistently side with extreme environmentalists who view jobs and a strong economy as the enemy of the environment. He had to consistently support raising energy taxes and limiting America's ability to produce more of its own energy.

All of these votes cast over many years in the Senate create a clear picture of John Kerry. He has a lot of priorities—but a strong economy and job growth are not among them.

There is something troubling about a politician spending his entire career promoting higher taxes and job-killing regulatory regimes and then when running for president telling folks that he will make jobs one of his top priorities. Voters will have several months to determine if this politician is speaking the truth.

Kerry, Chirac and Schroder: Ménage à Trois

(Originally published in June 2004)

Just months ago, John Kerry made headlines when he said, "I've met foreign leaders who can't go out and say this publicly, but they look at you and say, 'You've got to win this, you've got to beat [Bush]...'" When pressed to name the leaders, Kerry demurred.

Reporters subsequently discovered Kerry had not met with any world leaders during the campaign. But this commentary is not about whether Kerry is truthful. The more interesting question is why did Kerry think endorsements from anti-American foreigners would impress American voters?

Most Americans logically assumed Kerry was talking about French President Jacques Chirac and German Chancellor Gerhard Schroder. Why wouldn't these foreign leaders hope Kerry wins? Kerry has effectively promised to give France, Germany and the United Nations the power to determine if and when America can defend itself.

Kerry has sharply criticized Bush for not obtaining the approval of France, Germany and the UN for our war on terrorism. Kerry argues it is not legitimate for the United States to act unilaterally to protect itself. Instead, Kerry says the UN must "provide the necessary legitimacy..." Kerry has avoided explaining why he thinks the president of the United States needs the permission of France or the UN to defend America.

It is clear there were no circumstances under which France or the UN would have supported America in Iraq. France had negotiated too many secret, profitable and illegal business deals with Saddam Hussein. The UN was skimming millions from the "Oil for Food" program.

France and the UN did not oppose Bush because they thought his policy was wrong. They opposed him because his policy would expose their illegal dealings and end the flow of Saddam's blood money. With this in mind, why does Kerry criticize President Bush for not obtaining the support of France, the U.N and others? Why did Kerry think Americans would be impressed that disingenuous, anti-American foreign leaders supported him?

Perhaps it is because Kerry is part of the blame-America-first-crowd and Europe's anti-Americanism only reinforces his own views. Thus, he does not perceive their grotesque bias or their corruption. After all, John Kerry is no stranger to anti-American rants. He said, "Our democracy is a farce." And he made sweeping accusations against American Vietnam veterans, repeatedly calling them drug addicts, rapists, murderers and war criminals.

Watching France celebrate the recent sixtieth anniversary of D-Day—the U.S. led invasion to liberate Europe from German control—one was left to conclude the French liberated themselves. Nations who had nothing to do with France's liberation were given equal footing with America. Oddly, Chirac placed Germany above nations who spilt blood and spent treasure to liberate France from German domination. Schroder thanked France and Russia by name for liberating Germany from the German Nazis. But he could not bring himself to properly acknowledge America's indispensable leadership.

Chirac and Schroder implied France led the war effort. The truth is Germany rolled through France without any significant resistance. America, and to a lesser degree Britain, liberated France. The French simply were not a factor. They have not been an important world player since Napoleon's defeat two centuries ago. But to anti-American European minds, France liberated itself and Germany too and America was just a footnote.

These are the folks John Kerry is comfortable with. These are the people whose support Kerry seeks and values. The problem is these folks are so anti-American they cannot acknowledge what is obvious even to schoolchildren—America liberated France from Hitler's domination.

Americans should ask themselves if John Kerry would provide the sort of leadership America needs. Is America prepared to have a president whose worldview more closely resembles Jacques Chirac's than Ronald Reagan's? Kerry called Reagan's presidency one of "moral darkness" and bragged he was "proud" to have "stood against Ronald Reagan, not with him." Are we prepared to have a president that is more likely to please France than America?

Streisand, Moore and Fahrenheit 9/11

(Originally published in July 2004)

When I was a young boy, my mother taught me to choose my friends and associates carefully and warned me that others would judge me by the company I kept. This is almost universal advice and I suspect that John Kerry's mother gave him similar warnings. But apparently, John did not listen. Kerry's friends, supporters and associates include some very troubling and extreme people.

The Hollywood left, for example, just hosted a $5 million fundraiser for Kerry in Los Angeles. The same people, who glorify and sell sex, violence and counter-culture values to our children, endorse John Kerry and his leadership.

Barbra Streisand sang old favorites and told the crowd, who paid up to $25,000 each to attend, that Secretary of Defense Donald Rumsfeld is "the spookiest person in the world." John Kerry and the Hollywood crowd heartily approved. However, to most Americans, even those who have questions about Bush's policies or Rumsfeld's implementation of them, the threat of terrorism is far more "spooky" than a man who has served his country twice as Secretary of Defense. Most Americans understand that we are fighting a war on terror in the terrorist's backyard so that the battle is not fought on America's streets.

Those who hope to never see another day like September 11th are mighty glad that Mr. Rumsfeld is scary to terrorists. Being scary to terrorists is a good thing. This simple truth completely escaped Barbra Streisand, John Kerry and his adoring Hollywood supporters. It also escapes the French and other foreign leaders whose support John Kerry's claims.

But Hollywood's support doesn't end with fundraising. After much hoopla, Michael Moore's anti-Bush propaganda movie, *Fahrenheit 9/11*, opened in theatres. Moore calls it a "documentary," but in just the first few minutes of the movie, Moore's deception reaches breathtaking heights. First, Moore claims that Bush stole the presidency and that Gore won in Florida. Yet, several news organizations counted and recounted every single ballot in Florida and each time Bush won—regardless of the methodology used. These are the indisputable facts and they were available to Moore, but he simply ignored them.

Second, Moore falsely claims that Bush allowed bin Laden's relatives to return to Saudi Arabia shortly after September 11th on secret flights when the rest of the nation was grounded. However, Bush did no such thing. Richard Clarke, who now bashes Bush for the war on terror, admits he, not Bush, approved the flights.

But they weren't secret flights while the rest of the nation was grounded. Moore liberally uses Clarke's anti-Bush statements when they support his conspiracy theories, but when Clarke's testimony doesn't support his objectives, Moore edits Clarke out of the movie and simply makes up "facts." Moore doesn't allow the truth to get in his way.

The New York Times printed that Moore's movie was "an editorial cartoon." *The Los Angeles Times* said, "It is propaganda, no doubt about it." *The Washington Post* said the movie was "threaded…with cheap shots" and was essentially a "cartoon." The reviewer "was troubled by the cheapness of Moore's interviewing techniques." Fox News's Bill O'Reilly called it "rank propaganda." Even Michael Moore offers no defense, saying, "I'm not trying to pretend that this is some sort of, you know, fair and balanced work of journalism."

In the left-leaning *Slate Magazine*, Christopher Hitchens wrote, "To describe this film as dishonest and demagogic would almost be to promote those terms to the level of respectability. To describe this film as a piece of crap would be to run the risk of a discourse that would never again rise above the excremental. To describe it as an exercise in facile crowd-pleasing would be too obvious. *Fahrenheit 9/11* is a sinister exercise in moral frivolity, crudely disguised as an exercise in seriousness. It is also a spectacle of abject political cowardice masking itself as a demonstration of 'dissenting' bravery."

John Kerry counts as friends people who are more afraid of Donald Rumsfeld than murderous terrorists. Kerry's friends are people who have more anger towards the president than those who plot to kill, maim and behead Americans. Kerry has wide support in Hollywood where America-hating is not just sport, it is a badge of honor. The "blame America first crowd" is part of Kerry's bedrock of support. Streisand, Moore and Kerry's nameless foreign leader friends are only a few examples. This is the crowd that supports Kerry—anti-American foreign leaders and Hollywood extremists. What does that tell us about John Kerry? What would your mother say?

Redefining Values

(Originally published in July 2004)

When two Democratic pundits were recently asked whether John Kerry and John Edwards shared the values of regular, every day Americans, they of course answered, "Yes." Their answer was not surprising, but how they defined values was. To these Democratic spinmeisters, sharing the values of Americans meant being for restrictive environmental regulations that kill jobs but don't really make the environment safer or cleaner, increasing taxes and supporting government run healthcare. These are political issues, not values.

At first, I thought perhaps these pundits were unsure how to answer the values question. However, a few days later, a report stated Kerry and Edwards would campaign on values, but would redefine values so as not to give away the values issue to President George W. Bush. Then I realized these pundits had been doing precisely what the Kerry-Edwards campaign had instructed—don't talk about values. Instead, talk about political issues *as if they were values.*

Kerry and Edwards cannot campaign on values. They have voted against the Boy Scouts and in support of partial-birth abortion, public funding of abortion and gay marriage. They support ultraliberal judges who declare the Pledge of Allegiance unconstitutional, ban the mere mention of God and protect child pornography. They have obstructed confirmation of judges that virtually everyone else, including the liberal American Bar Association, say are qualified. All of this runs in direct conflict with America's values.

But they cannot publicly admit their values are out of touch with America. So when asked about values, they launch into how they agree with Americans on whatever issue they wish to discuss—the environment, healthcare, etcetera. But they will not discuss actual values.

John Kerry is the most liberal U.S. Senator as rated by the nonpartisan *National Journal.* John Edwards is the fourth most liberal Senator. This is the most liberal Democratic ticket ever. They make Ted Kennedy and Hillary Clinton look moderate, which is no small feat. They make Walter Mondale and Geraldine Ferraro look reasonable. Yet, the Mondale-Ferraro ticket was so liberal they lost in an embarrassing landside to Ronald Reagan and George Bush—winning only one state out of fifty. This is why Kerry and Edwards cannot acknowledge their anti-values record. This is why Kerry and Edwards are engaging in a great campaign of deception to convince voters that they share America's values.

Kerry and Edwards count as their friends and supporters the most extreme and counterculture of Hollywood's stars. At a recent fundraiser, stars entertained the attendees by liberally using the F-word, joking about women's genitalia and calling President Bush a murdering thug. John Kerry thanked his Hollywood buddies and said they represented the "heart and soul" of America and the values of Americans. The campaign collected a cool $5 million, but refuses to release video of the event. Why? To hide Kerry's counterculture values from public view. The very people who sell sex and violence to our youth are lining up to extol Kerry's values. And Kerry praises them as representing America's values. Kerry and Edwards are the counterculture, anti-values ticket.

John Kerry's values translate into taxpayer funding of abortion and abortion on demand—even minutes before an otherwise healthy birth. Kerry's values mean that gay marriage would have strong support in the White House, but the Boy Scouts would be opposed. Kerry's values mean he will appoint ultraliberal judges committed to the cultural overthrow of America. Thus, there will be more protection of child pornography, more attempts to ban the Pledge and more hostility towards God and religion. Kerry's values mean that government will have greater control over our children's education and parents less.

John Kerry and John Edwards have values, but they are not the values that my parents taught me or that I am teaching my children. Nor are they the values I see my neighbors teaching their children. John Kerry has evidently figured this out and determined that rather than talking about values, he'll change the subject and talk about something else. For voters who believe values matter, this should be very troubling.

An Honest Mistake?

(Originally published in July 2004)

Bill Clinton has not occupied the Oval Office for more than three years and John Kerry has not yet faced a national election, but both are potentially knee-deep in a serious scandal—and this one is not about sex. This one involves national security.

Sandy Berger—who was Clinton's National Security Advisor and who has been advising presidential candidate John Kerry on national security issues—admits that he removed highly classified and top-secret documents from a National Archives "safe room." He also admits that he subsequently discarded some of the top-secret documents. It is unknown whether America's enemies discovered the classified information Berger discarded.

Mr. Berger excuses this shocking breach of national security saying it was a "sloppy error" but an "honest mistake." Bill Clinton laughed it off because Berger often had stacks of paper all over his desk. John Kerry says that Berger is a trusted friend and questions the timing of these revelations. Other Democrats also question the timing.

Only John Kerry and his soft-on-national-security friends could respond to such a serious breach of security by asking, "Why now?" Perhaps Kerry can explain why now is a bad time for this story and when would be a better time. Kerry is apparently more concerned about the timing of the story than he is about the fact that his friend and his trusted advisor knowingly violated the safety of highly classified national security and anti-terrorism information.

Kerry's response is troubling and hints at much larger issues—not the least of which is whether Kerry is capable of pursuing America's vital national security interests over his own political ambitions.

It would be sloppy for Mr. Berger to accidentally remove top-secret documents. But media reports state that Berger hid the top-secret documents in his shorts and socks. It is almost unimaginable that this was the result of an "honest mistake" or even "sloppiness."

Perhaps even more damning is the fact that on two different days, Mr. Berger reportedly stuffed different drafts of the same document into his underwear and socks. Perhaps, top-secret documents can accidentally get stuffed into one's underwear once, but it seems impossible that the same documents, discussing the same issues, would find their way into Berger's "unmentionables" a second time.

Among the documents Berger reportedly hid twice in his underwear was a memo assessing al Qaeda threats, terrorism risks and Clinton's handling of terrorism. Rehashing Clinton's failures is not the point. What matters now is that we aggressively defeat al Qaeda and defend America. However, John Kerry's sad response to these revelations brings into question his ability and fitness to lead and defend America.

From the public testimony that was given before the 9/11 Commission, it appears that the memo purportedly found twice in Berger's underwear goes to the heart of whether we should treat terrorism as a "law enforcement" issue as John Kerry has repeatedly said, or whether it is a "national security" issue as George W. Bush has said. To Kerry, terrorists should be treated like liquor store robbers. To Bush terrorists and their allies should be treated like sworn enemies of America. This difference will be key in the election debate.

What in this memo was so interesting to John Kerry's security advisor? Why did Kerry's key advisor try to dispose of several drafts of the same memo? Why was such sensitive information dealt with so recklessly? Perhaps Kerry's advisor realized that John Kerry is vulnerable to charges of repeating Clinton's mistakes and of being soft on terrorism and soft on defense. Even a sitting Democrat, Senator Zell Miller, has warned that Kerry will outsource our national security to France and Germany. Perhaps, in an election year, this memo was simply too hot for John Kerry to handle and his friend and advisor was "sloppily" clearing a path for him.

Regardless, Kerry is more concerned about the timing of this matter than he is about the substance of it. This reveals that John Kerry lacks the ability to lead America in the war on terror and that he cannot be trusted to defend America's national security interests above all else.

Uppity Rich Guy with a Superiority Complex

(Originally published in July 2004)

John Kerry says he represents the forgotten regular folks. He campaigns in plaid shirts, brags to autoworkers that he proudly drives a truck, and shoots guns for the newsreel—all to convince voters that he's a regular guy. But it is not genuine. It's simply for show. The real John Kerry is an elitist patrician.

The dictionary defines patrician as "a member of an aristocracy." In modern usage, patrician means "uppity rich guy who thinks he's better than everyone." John Kerry is the poster boy for uppity rich guys with superiority complexes. Thus, his campaign is attempting an extreme makeover so that Kerry will appear as if he were a regular American who shares our values. This extreme character makeover will involve a lot more than botox.

In Boston, where the junior senator from Massachusetts lives when he's not skipping Senate votes, John Kerry stories are commonplace. Most of these stories involve Kerry pulling rank on a "little guy," cutting to the front of the line, expecting special treatment or demanding something for free. When confronted about his behavior, Kerry defiantly asks, "Do you know who I am?" Evidently, Kerry believes that once the "little people" understand how important he is, they will simply back down and shut up.

John Kerry went snow boarding this winter and when a reporter asked if he fell, he blamed a Secret Service agent for knocking him down and cursed him—calling him a "son of a b*tch." There was no evidence the Secret Service agent had accidentally knocked Kerry down, but even if he had, couldn't Kerry muster even a little respect for the man who was willing to take a bullet for him? By Kerry's way of thinking, a man risking his life to protect Kerry is just a "son of a b*tch."

His political allies and friends joke that John Kerry's initials, JFK, stand for "Just For Kerry" because he is self-absorbed and views himself as smarter and better than others.

This is why Kerry supports legislation to make it more difficult for regular American families to buy and drive SUVs and minivans, while he and his wife drive SUVs and will always be able to. This is why he brags to autoworkers that he drives American-made SUVs, but brags to environmentalists that he has led the charge to effectively ban SUVs and minivans because they're too big.

He demanded Boston move a fire hydrant from in front of his Beacon Hill mansion so that he could park his SUV there. His neighbors must live with the fire hydrant, but not John. He's too good for that.

John Kerry holds Americans in contempt. To Kerry (and the French), we are stupid fools. This explains why he says one thing and does another. Kerry rails against "influence-peddlers and special interests." Yet, the nonpartisan Center for Responsive Politics found that Kerry accepted more money from lobbyists than any other Senator over the past fifteen years.

Kerry denounces corporations and "Benedict Arnold CEOs [who] send American jobs overseas." But the wealth of his billion-dollar wife came from the Heinz Co., which operates twenty-two factories in America and fifty-seven in foreign countries where labor is cheap. Kerry says he believes life begins at conception, but has voted repeatedly in favor of partial-birth abortion.

Kerry's wife, Teresa Heinz Kerry, recently gave a speech about the importance of civility in political discourse in which she referred to some harsh political talk as un-American. Minutes later when asked by a reporter what she meant by "un-American," she denied saying it and left in a huff. A few minutes later, she returned to tell the reporter to "Shove it." So much for civil discourse. Later, she explained away her outburst by blaming the reporter and saying that she was simply trying to get him "out of [her] face." Yet, video of the incident reveals the reporter was never in her face and that she left the reporter without answering his question, only to return a couple of minutes later to tell the surprised reporter, "Shove it."

This is what patricians do—hold the "little guy" in contempt. They call the man who protects their life a "son of a b*tch." They cut in line and expect special privileges because they're more important. They say things that aren't true because they're smarter. When someone asks why they behave this way, the patrician demands, "Do you know who I am?" or tells them to "Shove it."

This is John Kerry's true character. An extreme makeover may not be sufficient.

What Kerry's Convention Didn't Say

(Originally published in August 2004)

The Democratic convention was surprising—not for what was said, but for what was not said. John Kerry has served in the U.S. Senate for two decades—during the Reagan years, the first Bush years, the Clinton years and the current Bush years. Someone should have mentioned Kerry's Senate record. Yet, virtually nothing was said about it.

During the convention, we were reminded virtually every few minutes that Kerry served four months in Vietnam. But Kerry's twenty-year Senate record received virtually no attention.

Many veterans question Kerry's military record and even more detest him for fanning the flames of hatred against returning Vietnam veterans with his false accusations of war crimes. I cannot dismiss their concerns, but I am willing to stipulate that during those four months in Vietnam, Kerry led his crew of six honorably and won recognition for his service.

I am not questioning what Kerry did in Vietnam. I am asking why the things Kerry has done since Vietnam did not receive more attention. Why did Kerry ignore his twenty years in the Senate?

Kerry lags far behind President George Bush in polls on the question of who will better defend America and defeat terror. Kerry must close that gap if he hopes to win the election. So why didn't Kerry use his twenty-year Senate career to prove he can be trusted to lead and defend America? Why only talk about four months in Vietnam?

Kerry's twenty-year Senate record shows that he does not have the vision or resolve to vigorously defend America. The focus on Vietnam was a diversionary tactic—to distract us from his Senate years.

Throughout his career, Kerry has cut defense and intelligence funding. One of the reasons we lacked good intelligence leading up to September 11th, was that during the 1980s and 1990s, Kerry helped gut our intelligence apparatus. Now he says we should trust him to rebuild it.

When communism was entrenched in Central America, Ronald Reagan fought to financially assist our neighbors to free themselves from the oppressive regimes. Kerry opposed freedom for our neighbors. Instead, he supported communist dictators and mass-murderers like Daniel Ortega and even called them "reformers." Today, there are free elections in Nicaragua. But, Kerry gets no credit. He opposed the very policies that helped democracy take root there. Kerry was on the wrong side of history.

When America liberated Grenada from the grasp of an oppressive communist regime, Kerry opposed it. Today, Grenada is a democracy. But Kerry can claim no credit. Again, he was on the wrong side of history.

When Soviet communism threatened America and most experts doubted America could defeat communism, Kerry shared their pessimism and supported appeasement. His goal was to get along with the communists, not defeat them. Kerry opposed deployment of upgraded missile systems to deter the Soviet threat. Kerry even opposed missile defense. Kerry opposed virtually every weapons system our armed forces currently use.

Reagan sought victory over communism. Kerry wanted co-existence. Soviet communism is now dead. The gulags are no more. Hundreds of millions of former Soviets now enjoy freedom. Soviet missiles no longer threaten America. But Kerry cannot claim credit. He was on the wrong side of history.

When Saddam Hussein invaded Kuwait, Kerry opposed liberation. A decade later, when the war in Iraq was voted on, Kerry reluctantly supported it. But only a few months later, Kerry voted against funding the troops in the field—voting against supplying needed body armor, equipment and supplies.

In defense of his vote, Kerry explains that he "voted for [funding the troops] before [he] voted against it." That is not the explanation of a decisive leader.

In a recent poll, the citizens of Massachusetts, who know John Kerry best, overwhelming said that if elected president, Kerry would cut defense, regardless of what he says now.

On important national defense issues, time after time Senator Kerry has been on the wrong side of history. Kerry has consistently sought something less than victory. Little wonder Kerry focused on his four months in Vietnam rather than his twenty years in the Senate.

"Reporting for Duty" and "Send Me"

(Originally published in August 2004)

To win the election, John Kerry must convince Americans that President George W. Bush is not doing enough to make America safe and that Kerry would be more aggressive in protecting America. Thus, Kerry began his convention speech by telling voters he was "reporting for duty" and focused on his four months in Vietnam while ignoring his twenty years in the Senate. When criticizing President Bush, Kerry claims Bush is doing both too little, and too much, to make America safer.

After the convention, Kerry dramatically stated almost three years have passed since the September 11th attacks and President Bush has waited far too long to implement the 9/11 Commission's recommendations. But Kerry's argument that Bush has acted slowly is revealed as cheap political theatrics when one considers the Commission's report was released just two weeks ago, not three years ago.

Even without the Commission's recommendations, President Bush has been quite busy since September 11, 2001. Bush pushed for the Patriot Act. He established the Department of Homeland Security. He implemented numerous security and intelligence reforms—now the FBI and CIA share intelligence and America's policy is to preemptively stop terrorist plots before they happen, rather than just react after the fact. Afghanistan, once a haven for al Qaeda terrorists, is now holding free elections. Saddam Hussein, a funder, supporter and collaborator with al Qaeda, now sits in a prison cell. Countless terrorist plans have been disrupted and prevented before they were carried out. Nonetheless, Kerry claims Bush has not been aggressive enough.

In the next breath, Kerry also criticizes President Bush for doing too much—arguing we have no business in Iraq. Kerry specifically criticizes President Bush for working to preemptively defeat terrorists and stop attacks before they happen. Conversely, Kerry promises, "any attack will be met with a swift and certain response." In other words, Kerry will respond *after* the attack, but he will not preempt it.

Just before the convention, Kerry cut short his briefing with the 9/11 Commission to attend a campaign breakfast. Kerry also skipped almost 90% of all Senate votes this year and about two-thirds of all votes last year so he could campaign. Precisely what does Kerry mean when he says he is "reporting for duty?"

Clearly Kerry is more interested in *campaigning* for the job than he is in *doing* the job.

Throughout his long political career, Kerry has consistently voted to slash America's intelligence and gut the military—voting against critical weapons systems and even missile defense. Now in an election year when national security is the top issue, Kerry tells America he is "reporting for duty." In direct opposition to his twenty-year Senate record, Kerry promises to "add 40,000" new troops and to "provide our troops with the newest weapons and technology." If Kerry really supports a strong military, where has he been the last twenty years? Or even the last twelve months? Why is he only "reporting for duty" now? Why report for duty only three months before the election?

At the convention, Bill Clinton told us whenever America needed leadership, Kerry said, "Send me." Clinton delivered the applause line well, but truth and accuracy have never been his strength. This is what we were not told. When Soviet-backed communist dictator, Daniel Ortega, needed an American politician to provide cover so that Ortega could strengthen his death gripe over a victimized people yearning for freedom, John Kerry said, "Send me." Kerry went to Nicaragua to meet with the murderous dictator and returned to America lauding Ortega as a reformer and calling for support of the communist regime in Central America.

When communist dictators in El Salvador needed a politician to give them similar support, John Kerry again said, "Send me."

John Kerry has not, and will not, honestly detail his Senate record. To win this election, Kerry must hide his twenty-year record of being soft on defense, appeasing our enemies and being on the wrong side of history. When Kerry says he is "reporting for duty," it is a fair question to ask where has he been for the last twenty years.

Foreign Leaders and Osama bin Laden

(Originally published in August 2004)

More than once, John Kerry has told voters that a few unnamed foreign leaders prefer him to George W. Bush as the President of the United States. Even John Edwards has repeated the foreign endorsement theme. Recently, Democratic Senators Joseph Biden and Carl Levin returned from Europe telling America that unnamed European leaders (presumably the French and Germans) stand ready to put their full weight behind our efforts in Iraq only if John Kerry resides in the White House. Subsequent reports now lay bare Kerry's silly claims—both the French and the Germans say there are no circumstances under which they will help in Iraq.

It is puzzling that Democrats think Americans should be impressed that anti-American foreign leaders support Kerry. As dubious as Kerry's claims of foreign endorsements may be, there is at least one foreign leader who hopes for a Kerry-Edwards win in November. However, even the two Johns are smart enough not to brag about having this foreign leader's support. Of whom am I speaking? Osama bin Laden.

If Osama bin Laden could vote in November and had to choose between President George W. Bush and Senator John Kerry, how would Osama vote? The answer couldn't be easier or clearer.

The last thing bin Laden and al Qaeda terrorists want is four more years of President George W. Bush's unyielding pounding. Thanks to Bush's leadership, Osama and his terrorists have been pursued relentlessly for almost three years—thousands driven and killed and captured as they hide in remote mountain caves. Al Qaeda's leadership has been decimated. Their network has been weakened and their plans disrupted. It's easy to understand why Osama would prefer a change at 1600 Pennsylvania Avenue.

Kerry has been highly critical of President Bush's uncompromising pursuit of terrorism and said that he would do things differently. That is precisely why Osama is hoping for a Kerry victory in November. Kerry has repeatedly said that terrorism should be dealt with as a "law enforcement" issue. Simply put, Kerry wants to arrest terrorists and have attorneys prosecute them. Little wonder Osama is pulling for Kerry.

For the record, president Bill Clinton tried the law enforcement approach the first time the World Trade Center was bombed by terrorists more than a decade ago. Ramzi Yousef now sits in prison for bombing the World Trade Center in 1993—killing six and wounding hundreds. We now know the "law enforcement" reactionary approach did nothing to protect America on September 11, 2001.

Kerry has repeatedly criticized Bush for preemptively fighting terrorism. Kerry says that he will react swiftly after the fact. In his convention speech, Kerry promised, "Any attack will be met with a swift and certain response." Simply stated, his own words make it clear that John Kerry will not preemptively fight terrorism. He will wait and react. We are supposed to take comfort that after another attack, Kerry will respond swiftly and certainly. I doubt the thought of a commander-in-chief who waits to respond to attacks rather than preempting them provides much comfort to most Americans. But Osama is certainly comforted.

Al Qaeda has stated that it would like to "influence" America's election as it did earlier this year in Spain. In March, the Spanish party in power, who supported America's war on terror, lost a very close election due to a terrorist attack just days before the election. Al Qaeda is reportedly planning similar attacks in America in hopes of defeating Bush in November.

Al Qaeda does not want four more years of Bush's relentless pursuit. To survive, the terrorists need a breather. Bush's doctrine of preemption will provide no respite. On the other hand, John Kerry will provide a much-needed breather by shifting from Bush's preemptive approach to a passive reactionary approach.

So next time Kerry or his surrogates boast that Kerry has support from foreign leaders, you can be sure that there is at least one foreign leader pulling for Kerry. This should comfort no one in America.

Dizzy on National Defense and Intelligence

(Originally published in August 2004)

John Kerry has spent the last year criticizing President George W. Bush for misleading America about Iraq and weapons of mass destruction (WMD). Kerry began this tactic once he saw Howard Dean pulling away in the early nomination phase. Oddly enough, before Dean's fiery anti-war rhetoric, Kerry could have been President Bush's spokesman on Iraq. During the late 1990s, Kerry called for ground troops to invade Iraq and criticized then president Clinton for not doing enough to force Saddam to disarm. But the prospect of losing the nomination to Howard Dean made a convert of Kerry.

Before Kerry was converted by Dean's success, Kerry said Saddam had weapons of mass destruction and that regime change was a noble goal. On September 23, 2001 on CBS's *Face the Nation*, Senator John Kerry said, "[I]t is something that we know…for instance, Saddam Hussein has used weapons of mass destruction against his own people, and there is some evidence of their efforts to try to secure these kinds of weapons and even test them."

On July 29, 2002, in New York City, Senator Kerry said, "I agree completely with [President Bush's] goal of a regime change in Iraq…Saddam Hussein is a renegade and outlaw who turned his back on the tough conditions of his surrender put in place by the United Nations in 1991."

If George Bush misrepresented the WMD risk or as some have accused him, if he lied about it, then John Kerry is the original WMD liar. John Kerry was "lying" about WMD in Iraq long before George Bush was president.

Kerry's defenders say he was just relying on mistaken intelligence. But that is also true of George Bush, Britain's Tony Blair, and Russia's Vladimir Putin to name only a few. Yet, somehow partisans claim Bush misled America while Kerry and everyone else justifiably relied on mistaken intelligence. That logic just doesn't work.

But maybe we can't blame Senator Kerry for relying on bad intelligence—for the eight years he was a member of the Senate Intelligence Committee, Kerry missed 76% of the public hearings. The year after the September 11th attacks, Kerry did not attend even one public hearing. For the record, President Bush attended 100% of his national security briefings.

But this goes deeper than skipping important hearings. Kerry also consistently voted to slash intelligence resources. In 1993, shortly after the first bombing of the World Trade Center, Senator Kerry proposed $7.5 billion in intelligence cuts. In 1994, he proposed another $6 billion in cuts to intelligence. Even fellow Democrats criticized the cuts as irresponsible and likely to hamstring future intelligence efforts. In 1995, Kerry again proposed intelligence cuts of $1.5 billion. Fortunately, not a single senator would co-sponsor his bill.

Since his Dean conversion, Kerry began arguing Bush should never have gone to war against Iraq. Then true to form, Kerry recently flip-flopped and says that he would have voted to authorize the war with Iraq even if he had known that there were no WMD.

Kerry's positions on Iraq and intelligence are terribly confusing. First, Kerry supports the war and calls for regime change in Iraq. Then, Kerry opposes the war, even telling MSNBC's Chris Matthews that he is the "antiwar candidate." Now, Kerry says he would have supported the war even if he had known there were no WMD. It is dizzying!

Throughout the 1990s Kerry tried to cut intelligence even when his fellow Democrats said no. Additionally, Kerry didn't attend intelligence hearings. Now Kerry says our intelligence apparatus needs an overhaul and he has the experience to do it. Yet, Kerry's experience is mostly skipping intelligence meetings for eight years and trying to slash intelligence resources. This is not the sort of "reform" most Americans are looking for.

Perhaps his dizzying record on the national defense and intelligence is why Kerry only wants to talk about his four months in Vietnam and ignore the specifics of his twenty-year Senate career.

An American Patriot: Zell Gave 'em Hell

(Originally published in August 2004)

The great hymn *America the Beautiful* defines patriots as those "who more than self their country loved..." In battle, patriotism causes soldiers to place themselves in harm's way to protect the liberty of those they love. In politics, patriotism causes men to love their country more than their party—greater concern for the national interest than for personal ambitions. Speaking at the GOP Convention, Senator Zell Miller, a life-long Democrat, proved himself an American patriot for the ages.

Senator Zell Miller has never before cast a vote for a Republican presidential candidate. He spoke at Bill Clinton's 1992 convention. He was Georgia's wildly popular Democratic Governor and now Senator. Many politicians reflexively defend their party, its positions, and its leaders—no matter how obviously wrong they may be. Not Zell Miller. He asks what is good for America rather than what helps him or his party politically. Zell Miller is an American patriot—a man "who more than self" his "country loves."

At the convention, Miller said, "the next four years will determine what kind of world [our children and grandchildren] will grow up in...I ask which leader is it today that has the vision, the willpower and, yes, the backbone to best protect my family?...For my family is more important than my party. There is but one man to whom I am willing to entrust their future and that man's name is George Bush."

Miller will win no friends in his party for his candor and straight talk. When he encounters fellow Democrats next week in the Senate, it will be a lonely and cold experience. But Americans should hail Zell Miller as a true patriot "who more than self" his "country loves."

Senator Miller rightly asked, "Where are the statesmen today?" He powerfully explained that protecting freedom was more important than attaining political office. He asked, "What has happened to the party I've spent my life working in?" His indictment followed—today's Democratic leaders are "motivated more by partisan politics than by national security."

A recent poll by the liberal Pew Center revealed that a majority of Democrats believe American foreign policy was partially responsible for the September 11th attacks. This is an astonishing belief which folks like John Kerry, Howard Dean, and Ted Kennedy have made acceptable. I suppose these same Democrats erroneously believe that women who wear short skirts or tight sweaters are partially responsible for their rape.

While Miller did not specifically address these outrageous poll findings, he criticized today's Democratic leadership because "they don't believe there is any real danger in the world except that which America brings upon itself through our clumsy and misguided foreign policy."

Senator Miller, who served his nation as a Marine, expressed righteous indignation that "today's Democratic leaders see America as an occupier, not as a liberator...Never in the history of the world has any soldier sacrificed more for the freedom and liberty of total strangers than the American soldier. And, our soldiers don't just give freedom abroad; they preserve it for us here at home...But don't waste your breath telling that to the leaders of my party today. In their warped way of thinking America is the problem, not the solution."

Senator Miller concluded by telling America, "For more than twenty years, on every one of the great issues of freedom and security, John Kerry has been more wrong, more weak and more wobbly than any other national figure...Right now the world just cannot afford an indecisive America. Fainthearted self-indulgence will put at risk all we care about in this world. In this hour of danger our president has had the courage to stand up. And this Democrat is proud to stand up with him."

Tom Daschle, Ted Kennedy and John Kerry won't stand with their fellow Democratic Senator Zell Miller. The truth he spoke in New York hits too close to home. They will dismiss and discount him. But America is fortunate, indeed, to have a fearless patriot like Zell Miller "who more than self" his "country loves." America stands with Zell.

What Do the Conventions Mean?

(Originally published in September 2004)

After the Democratic National Convention, polls indicated that John Kerry received no discernable bounce in the polls. Even Michael Dukakis, another Massachusetts liberal who lost in 1988 by landslide proportions, left his convention with a sizeable seventeen-point lead. So what happened? Kerry's spinmiesters explained that there was no bounce because the nation is closely divided and there simply are not enough undecideds to sway. That explanation quickly became conventional wisdom.

The bounce Bush received from the Republican Convention proves the conventional wisdom was dead wrong. If there were so few undecideds, why did Bush jump out to an eleven-point lead in the polls? Why did Kerry fail to win over undecideds where Bush succeeded?

At the Democratic Convention in Boston, Kerry told us he was "reporting for duty." His message was that he would be a better commander-in-chief due to his four months in Vietnam. Kerry strictly avoided discussing his twenty-year Senate career or his thirty years since Vietnam. It was as if Kerry was born, went to Vietnam for four months and then suddenly was running for president. Undecideds asked themselves, "Why is he reporting for duty only now? Where has he been the last twenty or thirty years?"

It turns out Kerry's record over the last twenty or thirty years does not support his claim that he would be a more effective and decisive commander-in-chief. On intelligence gathering, Kerry's approach has been to cut intelligence spending year after year and to skip 76% of Intelligence Committee public hearings over eight years and to skip all of such hearings the year after the September 11th attacks. Yet, Kerry claims he's the man to reform intelligence.

On defense, Kerry's approach has been to oppose virtually every major weapons and defensive system that we now use—even missile defense. Kerry's position on Iraq changes with every poll. Kerry has repeatedly promised to respond if attacked, but not to prevent attacks. Yet, Kerry says he is the man to lead America against terror.

On diplomacy, Kerry derides our most loyal allies and mocks their sacrifice calling them a coalition of "the coerced and bribed." Yet, Kerry promises to be more diplomatic and to build stronger relationships with our historically disloyal allies.

The undecideds looked at these facts and evidently were not impressed.

At the Republican National Convention, a life long Democrat, a popular former Governor of Georgia and a sitting U.S. Senator named Zell Miller explained why John Kerry could not be trusted to protect America. Senator Miller's own party has excoriated him for speaking the truth. But I am grateful that Senator Miller is an American first, and a Democrat second. That is statesmanship and it makes Senator Miller a profile in courage.

Miller reminded Americans that in the past national security had never been a partisan issue. He said, "Time after time in our history, in the face of great danger, Democrats and Republicans worked together to ensure that freedom would not falter. But not today. Motivated more by partisan politics than by national security, today's Democratic leaders see America as an occupier, not a liberator. And nothing makes this Marine madder than someone calling American troops occupiers rather than liberators…"

Miller continued, "Never in the history of the world has any soldier sacrificed more for the freedom and liberty of total strangers than the American soldier…No one should dare to even think about being the commander-in-chief of this country if he doesn't believe with all his heart that our soldiers are liberators abroad and defenders of freedom at home. But don't waste your breath telling that to the leaders of my party today. In their warped way of thinking, America is the problem, not the solution…For more than twenty years, on every one of the great issues of freedom and security, John Kerry has been more wrong, more weak and more wobbly than any other national figure."

The undecideds listened to Kerry and were unimpressed. They listened to Miller and realized that America needs a decisive, proactive commander-in-chief. Thus, Bush received a strong convention bounce, where Kerry received none. So much for conventional wisdom.

Election 2004: Lessons Learned so far...

(Originally published in September 2004)

It is less than two months until Election Day. What do we know so far? Here are some thoughts.

First, the debate on national security is over. Bush won and Kerry lost. The Democratic Convention in Boston was designed from top to bottom to paint Kerry as a war hero and a capable commander-in-chief. Kerry told us he was "reporting for duty." He focused almost exclusively on his four months in Vietnam. But after months of campaigning on being a more capable commander-in-chief and a week of convention prime time television coverage, it was clear that undecided voters were not buying it.

Now George Bush has up to an eleven-point lead and a 2-to-1 lead on the question of who will better lead America in the war on terror. Former President Bill Clinton and other party leaders have advised Kerry to move on to domestic issues. The national security debate is over and George Bush won.

Second, John Kerry's virtual refusal to discuss his twenty-year Senate career has left him wide open to being defined by his opponents. If Kerry plans to win, he must do the defining and not leave it to the opposition.

To date, most Americans only know that John Kerry is more liberal than Ted Kennedy; that he served four months in Vietnam, won medals, and accused his fellow soldiers of being war criminals; and that he can't make up his mind on key issues like Iraq and the war on terror.

Kerry has been the junior senator from Massachusetts for twenty years. There must be something in his career that is worth mentioning. If Kerry continues to avoid discussing his Senate record, Americans will logically conclude that he is ashamed of it—after all, he's had no hesitation to brag about his four months in Vietnam. Kerry should start bragging about his twenty-year political career in the Senate or he will lose.

Third, John Kerry's habit of doing one thing and saying another, and saying one thing and then saying another is only reinforcing the perception that he is an indecisive and unprincipled vacillator. Kerry needs to pick his issues better. He needs to find issues where he has a strong track record of leadership and a consistent position. But perhaps that is the problem.

Here are three examples where the issues on which Kerry campaigns actually reinforce his opposition's message and harm Kerry.

First, Kerry campaigns telling Americans that he is the man to reform our intelligence apparatus. Yet, during his Senate career, Kerry tried almost annually to cut intelligence spending. He skipped 76% percent of Intelligence Committee public hearings over an eight-year span and attended no such hearings for an entire year after September 11th.

Second, Kerry claims he would be a better commander-in-chief and lead America in the war on terror. Yet, for twenty years in the Senate, Kerry opposed virtually every major weapons and defensive system that we now use. He has consistently opposed missile defense. Kerry stridently opposed Reagan's policies—the very policies that led to the fall of communism. Kerry's position on Iraq changes with every poll. Kerry has repeatedly promised to respond *if* attacked, but not to prevent attacks. He voted for funding the troops in Iraq, "before [he] voted against it."

Third, Kerry claims he would be a better diplomat and would more effectively build alliances. Yet, he mocks our current allies calling them the "coalition of the coerced and bribed" and discounts their contribution and sacrifice. He is prepared to discard our most loyal allies in hopes of developing better relationships with those who have never been our long-term, reliable allies. It simply doesn't make sense to talk of being a better diplomat while disparaging our most loyal allies.

Kerry needs to talk about issues where he hasn't been all over the map or been demonstrably wrong during his senate career. Perhaps he is telling us there are no such issues.

Does this mean the election is over and that Bush is guaranteed to win? Of course not. In politics, anything can happen and six weeks in politics is a virtual eternity. But if Kerry continues to campaign as he has the last three months, he will lose and by more than the polls currently show. If Kerry can't find something in his twenty-year Senate career worth campaigning on, he will continue to serve as America's most liberal senator.

Presidential Leadership, Security and Honesty

(Originally published in September 2004)

A recent *ABC News/Washington Post* poll bodes very poorly for John Kerry. Not only does the poll show George Bush leading Kerry by a 52%-to-43% margin, but also on virtually every measure of leadership, honesty and personal appeal Kerry trails Bush by a sizeable margin.

On the question of who is a "strong leader," likely voters favored Bush over Kerry by a whopping 27 points (58%-to-31%). When asked who has a "clear stand on the issues," Bush again had a 27-point advantage (56%-to-29%). Voters have learned that Kerry's stand on an issue is like the weather or the wind—if you don't like it, be patient. It will change.

The war in Iraq is only one example of Kerry's dizzying record. Kerry initially voted to authorize military force in Iraq. Then once Howard Dean made being anti-war popular, Kerry proclaimed himself the anti-war candidate. Recently, Kerry flipped again saying if the vote were held today, he would again vote to authorize the war. But only days later, Kerry argued that Bush was wrong to go to war in Iraq. By Kerry's own admission, he "actually did vote for the $87 billion [to fund American troops in Iraq] before [he] voted against it."

As a child, I played with spinning tops that did not turn that quickly or frequently.

On the question of who "will make the country safer," Bush leads by 19 points (54%-to-35%). This should not come as a surprise. Kerry's entire twenty-year Senate career has been anti-military and anti-intelligence. He has consistently been wrong on arms control, missile defense and weapons and defensive systems. He has consistently supported cutting military and intelligence spending. At his convention, Kerry said if elected president, "Any attack will be met with a swift and certain response." In other words, Kerry will *respond* to attacks after the fact, but not prevent them. America has heard John Kerry loud and clear—this is why Bush leads.

Perhaps the worst news for Kerry is that on the question of who is "honest and trustworthy," Bush has a 13-point lead (48%-to-35%) and on the question of who has an "appealing personality" Bush leads by 22 points (53%-to-31%). If Americans do not believe they can trust Kerry and if they do not find him appealing, he will have a difficult time making the case that he should be president. Voters will simply tune him out.

Kerry's trustworthiness deficit is a problem of his own making. Part of the problem is his dizzying flip-flops on the issues. But Kerry's ever-changing explanations of his past are also a part of the problem—war protests during Vietnam, accusing American soldiers of systematic and widespread war crimes, throwing away medals and explaining his senate votes.

Kerry's personality deficit is the result of his uppityness. His long habit of pulling rank on the "little guy" is coming back to bite him—cutting in line, expecting special treatment or demanding something for free, and indignantly asking "Do you know who I am?" Last winter, after a day of snowboarding Kerry was asked if he fell. He answered, "I don't fall" and then blamed a Secret Service agent for knocking him down. That was ungracious enough, but then he called the Secret Service Agent a "son of a b*tch." Whether Kerry was accurate about his fall cannot be substantiated. But regardless, can't Kerry muster even a little respect for the man who would die to protect his life? This condescending attitude comes across loud and clear on the campaign trail. Little wonder voters don't find Mr. Kerry "an appealing personality."

Bush's current 9-point lead does not guarantee he will win on Election Day. There is time for Kerry to turn things around. But, Kerry's real problems are the major questions about his ability to lead, his willingness to defend America, his honesty and his personal appeal. He has less than two months to change the perceptions he has built over the last twenty to thirty years. That is no small challenge.

Debate Gaffes Doom Election Chances

(Originally published in October 2004)

Presidential debates are important. They can make a difference—gaffes can be deadly. For Senator John Kerry, the good news is that he looked and sounded good during the first presidential debate. The bad news is that he did not say anything that will attract undecided voters or peel off President George W. Bush's voters. The really bad news is that Kerry made three serious gaffes that virtually ensure his defeat.

Let's start with the good news. Kerry's "tan-in-a-can" orange glow had calmed down enough that he looked reasonably good. His $250 haircut was nice. He spent the afternoon before the debate getting a manicure, which evidently helped him appear rested and relaxed at the debate. It was difficult to see on television, but his hands must have looked great.

Seriously, Kerry was helped—as all challengers are—by standing on the same stage with the President and sharing the venue. Kerry looked relaxed and surprisingly kept his answers short. He successfully avoided sounding like the shrieking Howard Dean.

On style and presentation, Kerry won. Bush was okay, but not energetic enough. Kerry was smooth. Bush will never be a smooth talker. With the sound off, Kerry looked better. So Kerry gets the nod for presentation. The bad news for Kerry is that he was weak on substance, which was Bush's strength.

Kerry misrepresented the facts numerous times. For example, he charged that Bush diverted forces from Afghanistan to Iraq. Yet, the commander of both the Afghanistan and Iraq operations, now retired Gen. Tommy Franks, has unequivocally stated that is false. Kerry asserted that Iraq has cost more than $200 billion. But that is almost double the actual cost as determined by the nonpartisan Congressional Budget Office.

Kerry disingenuously denied that he had ever accused Bush of lying about Iraq, but on at least two occasions Kerry has said Bush "lied." One such incident was reported in Kerry's hometown newspaper. Kerry also asserted that President Bush hasn't made bridges and subways safer and provided as evidence that "they had to close down the subway in New York when the Republican Convention was there." But the subway was not closed. I rode the subway during the convention.

Aside from the false "facts" Kerry used, he had a bigger problem. In 90 minutes of debate, Kerry never said anything that would significantly expand his support beyond his current base. Kerry continues to try to have it both ways—calling it "the wrong war" and "a catastrophic mistake" and also telling us that he can do it better. Do what better? The wrong war? The catastrophic mistake? His loyal supporters will give him a pass, as will the "mainstream" media, but most Americans will be unwilling to trust the safety of their children to a man who can't make up his mind about whether deposing Saddam was a good or bad.

Kerry continually referred to having a better "plan" than President Bush, but never described it in clear, unambiguous terms. Beyond knowing that Kerry believes Bush has made big mistakes, it is not clear what Kerry thinks should be done. As nearly as I can tell, he plans to do what President Bush is doing—train Iraqi defense forces and quell the terrorists who are trying to disrupt the upcoming elections. Only Kerry promises to do it better. That is a rhetorical line, but it is not a plan.

Kerry was very clear, however, in stating that summits were a big part of his plan. Kerry said, "I know I can do a better job in Iraq. I have a plan to have a summit with all of the allies." When asked how he would resolve problems in Iraq, North Korea and elsewhere in the world, Kerry promises more meetings. President Bush has held such summits, but more importantly, Bush has taken action. Bush understands that terrorists don't respond to meetings. Kerry hasn't figured this out yet.

Another bad exchange for Kerry came when he criticized President Bush for holding multilateral negotiations with North Korea and said that America should pursue "bilateral" negotiations. In other words, Kerry criticized Bush for organizing a coalition of nations to put pressure on North Korea to behave properly. Instead, Kerry said the United States should have acted alone in discussions with North Korea. So according to Kerry, one of Bush's biggest mistakes in Iraq was not having a strong coalition and "going it alone." But in North Korea, Bush's mistake is having a strong coalition and not going it alone. Perhaps this explains why Kerry is widely viewed as a politician who will say anything to get elected.

Each time Kerry said, "I've had one position, one consistent position" on Iraq, he reminded Americans of three things—(1) that Kerry vacillates almost weekly on Iraq, (2) that even during the debate, Kerry never outlined a clear, unambiguous plan for Iraq or for America's security, and (3) that Kerry has vacillated so much and for so long he has grown blind to his habit.

Kerry excused his vote against the $87 billion to supply body armor and other supplies to our troops in Iraq by saying, "when I talked about the $87 billion, I made a mistake in how I talked about the war." Kerry thought his rehearsed sound bite was clever. But he missed the point. His mistake was not how he *talked*, but how he *voted*. His *words* were not the problem. His *vote*—to deny troops in the field body armor, vehicle armor and other needed supplies—was the problem.

Even Kerry once understood this. One month before he voted against the $87 billon, CBS asked how he would vote on the troop-funding bill. He responded, "I don't think any senator is going to abandon our troops and recklessly leave Iraq to whatever follows...That's irresponsible...I don't think anyone in the Congress is going to not give our troops ammunition, not give our troops the ability...to defend themselves. We're not going to cut and run..." Obviously, John Kerry's word doesn't mean much because only a month later he voted precisely as he said no responsible senator would.

Kerry said throughout the debate "the president made a mistake in invading Iraq." But when asked if "Americans are now dying in Iraq for a mistake?" Kerry said, "No." Which is it? If Kerry is correct that the war is a mistake, then anyone who has died fighting that war died for a mistake. But, John Kerry wants to have it both ways—be for *and* against the war. This is not leadership and America knows it. If Kerry meant to convince us that he is ready to lead America, he missed the mark.

Kerry asserted Bush is wasting billions in Iraq that could be better spent in America on health care and prescription drugs. But then he tried to reassure us, "I'm not talking about leaving. I'm talking about winning." Which is it? Spend the money on health care or win the war? Take your pick, Senator, but you can't have it both ways.

Kerry continued to argue that he would be a more effective diplomat than Bush, but Bush shot that claim down rather easily. Bush asked how Kerry could rally foreign leaders to help in Iraq when Kerry has called it a "catastrophic mistake," and the "wrong war at the wrong time." Why will foreign leaders who haven't helped us yet, suddenly commit their nation's blood and treasure to help in an action Kerry has repeatedly condemned as a mistake and a waste?

Kerry has shamefully belittled our most loyal allies, calling them the "coalition of the coerced and bribed." Additionally, when Iraq's Interim Prime Minister Ayad Allawi spoke to a joint session of Congress to report on progress in Iraq, Kerry didn't attend, but pushed his way onto camera to blast Allawi for not grasping how bad things are in Iraq. Kerry's campaign even mocked Allawi as a "puppet." Most Americans understand you can't belittle and mock your allies and then claim to be a better diplomat.

But Kerry's biggest problem is that he made a number of serious gaffes that will haunt him in the campaign and significantly contribute to his defeat.

First, Kerry criticized President Bush for not having a plan in Iraq, saying, "You don't take America to war unless you have the plan to win the peace. You don't send troops to war without the body armor that they need." Later, he said, "Help is on the way." This was a huge blunder. Kerry voted against the $87 billion to fund body armor and supplies for the troops. By his own admission, he was registering a "protest vote" over a tax cut he disliked. We are to conclude that the man asking us to trust him with the safety of our families thinks it is okay to deny body armor and other needed supplies to our troops because he didn't get his way on a tax bill? Little wonder folks don't trust Kerry to defend them.

Second, Kerry's discussion of nuclear proliferation revealed a shocking "blame-America-first" bias. He started his answer by correctly identifying the danger of nuclear proliferation among rogue nations. But then Kerry went on to lament that America is conducting research on "bunker-busting nuclear weapons" as if America cannot be trusted with such things. It is self-evident why Iran and North Korea should not have nuclear weapons. But why would Kerry object to America's continued research on such things? America is a fundamentally good and responsible nation. Currently, Iran and North Korea are not. We protect and liberate. Others enslave and dominate. It is alarming that John Kerry does not understand this distinction. It is reason enough for Americans to reject him out of hand.

Third, when asked what he thought of a preemptive war, Kerry said he would "do it in a way that passes the test, that passes the *global test*..." Kerry came right out and said what most Americans already feared—John Kerry will protect America *only if* the rest of the world approves.

President Bush didn't think much of Kerry's "global test." Bush stated, "My attitude is you take preemptive action in order to protect the American people." Period. No global tests. That is the election. Kerry says he'll protect America *if* France says he can. Bush will protect America, regardless of what foreign leaders say. If voters understand this difference, the election is over and it won't be close.

America is not going to elect a man who believes he must satisfy "global tests" before protecting our families from another September 11th. America is not going to elect a man who believes America cannot be trusted with new "bunker-buster" bombs. America is not going to elect a man who believes it is acceptable to register a protest by voting to deny the troops the supplies they need to defend themselves and protect America.

The bottom line is that Kerry did an excellent job securing the left wing of his party. He also probably secured roughly 44% of the vote in the general election. And he did it all with style. But that's not enough to get him elected.

Democratic Politics Make Professional Wrestling Look Genuine

(Originally published in October 2002)

The United States Supreme Court has said it will not get involved in the political food fight that started when Senator Robert Torricelli (D-NJ) abruptly pulled out of the election. So, what was all the fuss about? Giving voters a choice? Or allowing a political party to cling to power?

Senator Torricelli, also known as the "Torch" for his heated rhetoric, surprised everyone by announcing his withdrawal from the U.S. Senate race in New Jersey. He recognized what the polls have been saying for several weeks—he was losing badly.

Months ago, voters chose Torricelli to run for the Senate. He had a sizable lead and victory looked easy. But Senate investigations into political corruption became public. His own party reprimanded him. Torricelli's support collapsed. When given a choice between a corruption-tarnished Torricelli and a clean newcomer named Doug Forrester, the voters chose Forrester.

Since voters weren't choosing him, Torricelli dropped out of the race about one month before Election Day and well after the statutory deadline for adding new candidates to the ballot. Torricelli argued that voters have the right to choose between two candidates and that the courts must disregard established law and place a more electable name on the ballot. Never mind that there were several other names on the ballot, Torricelli went to court in the name of voter choice.

This line of argument is so absurdly silly, one can only laugh. But, alas, the New Jersey Supreme Court apparently has quite a sense of humor—as it ruled in Torricelli's favor. At the risk of insulting the intelligence of school children, here is where the Torch and the court slipped up legally, intellectually and constitutionally.

First, voters chose Torricelli to run for reelection to the Senate. He liked that choice. After months of news about corruption, he was down in the polls by landslide numbers. People were making a choice. They did not like corruption and they no longer liked the Torch. He did not like the voter's choice this time. So Torricelli withdrew from the race and demanded that voters be given another choice—one that he would like, presumably. Torricelli didn't care that voters have choices. He just wanted them to make choices he liked.

Second, there is no right to choose between two major party candidates. Every election year, there are hundreds of elections with only one candidate. This does not violate the rights of voters. Voters have a right to cast their ballot for whomever they please. They can even write-in their vote. With or without Torricelli or a replacement on the ballot, voters have an infinite number of choices.

Third, legislatures make the law about how elections will operate, not courts. Just because the law does not suit one's political objectives is not an excuse for the court to ignore or rewrite the law. Here's one right the Torch and the court never mentioned—the right to participate in orderly and fair elections with established rules and procedures. This right has been trampled under the guise of voter choice.

Fourth, the real question is whether a political party can—contrary to the law—replace a losing candidate after months of campaigning and only a few weeks before the election. Imagine the confusion if parties could switch candidates at the last minute simply to avoid losing. If this right exists, how many times can a losing candidate be replaced? May other parties replace losing candidates at the last minute demanding that voters have a choice? Where does it stop?

Voter choice or political power? The answer is clear. Shame on the Democrats, the Torch and the court.

Memo to the GOP

(Originally published in November 2002)

In the wake of the tragic death of Senator Paul Wellstone (D-Minn.), Minnesota voters have had less than one week to become acquainted with the "replacement" candidate who will appear on the ballot. Ordinarily, one week would not be enough time to learn about a candidate and his views.

But fortunately, the "replacement" candidate is not new. Voters remember Walter Mondale. Almost forty years ago, in 1964, Mondale was first appointed to the U.S. Senate. He served as Jimmy Carter's Vice president. In 1984, he ran for president against Ronald Reagan—losing an incredible 49 of 50 states. Since that landslide defeat, he has been in virtual political retirement.

Early polls suggest that Mondale has a small lead over his Republican opponent, Norm Coleman. Some pundits suggest that with only days until the election, Coleman cannot overcome Mondale's initial, but modest, lead. Whether these pundits are correct depends largely on what the GOP and Coleman do.

Republicans have a history of playing politics poorly. Democrats on the other hand generally excel at the political game. They play like they mean to win. Republicans often play like they hope to win.

The political rally billed as a "memorial service" is a prime example. Democrats ran the so-called memorial service like a political convention—complete with mega-screen television monitors, bare-knuckled partisan speeches smearing opponents, frenzied cheers for Democrats, hardy boos for Republicans, and wild political chants of "We will win. We will win…" It was a wonderful political rally, but as a memorial service, it was stunningly crass and offensive.

Democratic officials apparently don't care about Paul Wellstone or his memory nearly as much as they enjoy playing hardball politics and flimflamming their way to three hours of free television coverage. They play to win—even if they must trample the memory of their fallen hero and deceive the press and the public to do so.

What must Norm Coleman and Republicans do to win the election? They don't need to call Mondale names. They just need to repeatedly show the voters Mondale being Mondale.

First, Republicans must show Mondale in 1984 saying that in a time of economic weakness, he desperately wanted an $85 billion tax increase. As a Senator, Mondale voted for tax increases at least 16 times. Mondale defended his tax hike proposals by asserting that he was simply being honest. This time, Republicans should not be surprised if Mondale is less candid about his lifelong support for higher taxes.

Second, Republicans must remind voters of Mondale's weak record on fighting terrorism and protecting American interests in the Middle East. The last time he held office, during the Carter-Mondale administration, Americans were held hostage for 444 days in Iran by terrorists. The Carter-Mondale team never mustered a serious response to the crisis. Only the election of a new administration finally brought the crisis to an end and the hostages home.

Third, Republicans must remind voters of Mondale's poor economic record. During the Carter-Mondale years, America suffered steep inflation, staggering interest rates, soaring unemployment and record economic stagnation. As a result, a new word was born to describe a new economic low—stagflation. The Carter-Mondale administration did little more than blame Americans for a "malaise."

Walter Mondale first went to the U.S. Senate four decades ago. Mondale's ideas have been tried. The results weren't pretty. Perhaps over the years, voters have forgotten about the high taxes, the economy flat on its back and the weak and ineffectual national security policy. If the Republicans mean to win, they must remind voters of these facts. If they merely hope to win, anything will do.

Sound Policy and Leadership beat Political Gamesmanship

(Originally published in November 2002)

What can be learned from the 2002-midterm elections? Sound public policy and leadership beats good political gamesmanship. Time-proven historical trends say that the political party that occupies the White House will lose seats during a midterm election. Accordingly, the GOP should have lost seats in both Houses of Congress. But the Republicans bucked historical trends and gained seats in the House and the Senate because they presented the nation with an understandable plan on national security and the economy. Much of this was due to President George W. Bush's strong leadership.

On national security, the president vigorously pressed the war on terrorism and tried to reorganize the federal government's homeland defense apparatus to meet and defeat the new threat. On the economic front, the president championed tax cuts to pump more dollars into the lagging economy, and spur investment and job growth. By all accounts his plans appear to be working.

Despite midterm election historical trends being on their side, Democrats lost seats in the House and lost their temporary majority in the Senate. Why? Because their leadership began by reflexively opposing the president and then, as their polls soured and the election grew closer, they changed their tone but not their obstructionist ways—hoping to look better to voters. Thus, Democrats relegated themselves to being either an echo or a contrarian voice.

But Democrats provided no leadership despite their Senate majority. They refused hearings and floor votes to a record number of appellate judge nominees despite the America Bar Association's highest possible rating. On taxes, they claimed it was "irresponsible" to allow you and me to keep more of our own paycheck at a time when we need it most. On homeland defense, they claimed to support the president, but bottled up his homeland security bill because pandering to union special interests was more important than national security.

Voters are not stupid. When Tom Daschle opposed virtually everything Bush proposed—tax cuts, making energy affordable and reliable, creating a department of homeland defense, etcetera—he was playing a high stakes game of partisan politics. Voters clearly did not appreciate that he was gambling their economic future and the nation's security in an attempt to impede and embarrass the president.

Americans don't mind honest disagreement, but when the disagreement is based on political expediency rather than principle, voters are apt to punish the scoundrels. And that is what voters did on Election Day. They punished the party who was behaving badly and putting political ambitions and partisan interests ahead of the national interest.

Democrats in their zeal to score political victories and maintain their power base, turned off voters around the country—far beyond the states where the chicanery took place. Here are two examples.

In Minnesota, Democrats were so intent on grabbing whatever advantage they could that they trashed the memory of their fallen hero, Senator Paul Wellstone, by turning his memorial service into a raucous political rally—complete with crowd cheers and chants of, "We will win. We will win…" and roof-raising boos for any recognizable Republican who attended the service to pay respects to the fallen colleague. If you can't be civil at a funeral, you can't be civil anywhere.

This grotesque display angered middle-of-the-road voters nationwide and gave them an ugly view of the Democratic Party and its "vision" for the future. Walter Mondale emphasized this incivility during the race's lone debate by returning his opponent's respectful and civil tone with rudeness, finger wagging and name-calling. The impact of this ugliness was felt far beyond the state lines of Minnesota.

New Jersey presented a vivid example of the lawless depths to which Democrats are willing to descend in their attempt to cling to power. New Jersey law clearly and unambiguously provides that once the election was only a few weeks away, new candidates cannot be placed on the ballot simply because the first candidate is losing and wants to withdraw. There is good reason for this. Voters must be given the opportunity to closely examine candidates over an extended period of time and in a variety of circumstances. However, Democrats decided just a few weeks before the election—even though the statutory deadline for adding candidates had long since passed—that they would ask the courts to ignore the law and order their replacement candidate be placed on the ballot.

Once the incumbent Senator, Robert Torricelli, understood that the voters were no longer choosing him, he withdrew and argued the law must be broken so that voters would have a choice. Yet, it was precisely because the voters were exercising their choice that Torricelli had gone from being a sure winner in the summer to a sure loser on election day. Moreover, there were other candidates on the ballot and an infinite number of write-in choices. Choice was never the issue. It was all about power.

A politically corrupt New Jersey court sided with Torricelli and disregarded the law and effectively legislated from the bench to create a new set of rules and procedures. Some New Jersey voters were embarrassed by the win-at-any-cost tactics and justifiably so. But nationwide, voters saw more evidence that Democrats have no plan for the future. They simply wanted to retain power and were breaking the law to do it. The illegal last-minute replacement candidate may have won the senate election in New Jersey, but the unbridled cynicism of this event further eroded the Democrat's credibility nationwide.

What will Republicans learn from this election? Republicans have a long history of playing political games poorly. Perhaps they will learn that strong leadership and good policy are good politics. Good substance beats good form every time.

What will Democrats learn? Not much, if Tom Daschle's recent performance is any indication. Daschle blamed the poor election results on talk radio which he said had encouraged hatred and had endangered him and his family. To blame the election results on talk radio is like a college football coach blaming his team's losing record on the callers to the coach's after game call-in show. While I do not always agree with what I hear on talk radio or news programs, I have never heard anyone encourage hatred or violence against Tom Daschle, his family or anyone else.

Voters rejected Tom Daschle's politics because he was politically extreme and partisan. Members of his own party warned that his extremism and partisan obstructionism were bad for America and would hurt Democrats. Daschle ignored them and paid the price on election day. Rather than blaming his problems on radio programs, Daschle should work with the president to make America stronger, freer and more prosperous. If he had done this throughout 2002, Daschle might still be the Majority Leader.

2

The Environment, Conservation and Junk Science

From Ice Age to Warming: What's Next?

(Originally published in September 2000)

Al Gore urges Americans to adopt environmental protection as "the central organizing principle for civilization" even before the facts on global warming are known. "Research in lieu of action is unconscionable," he says. Maybe. But wouldn't research help us learn what action, *if any*, is required?

Perhaps Mr. Gore prefers not to look at the scientific data because it does not support his political agenda. Gore argues that increased carbon dioxide (CO_2) emissions are causing global warming. But, the facts do not support this assertion. First, the earth's temperature naturally fluctuates. Second, roughly 80% of the carbon dioxide about which Mr. Gore complains was emitted *after* 1940. Yet, most of the 0.5° C "warming" Mr. Gore blames on carbon dioxide emissions occurred between 1850 and 1940—after several centuries of cooling known as the Little Ice Age. If the one-half degree warming occurred before the carbon dioxide was emitted, then the carbon dioxide could not have caused the warming. It's called cause-effect for a reason. The sequence matters. Third, Gore and his allies often incorrectly imply that carbon dioxide is a pollutant, when it is a gas that humans breathe in and out and plants must have to sustain life.

Yet, Al Gore says the scientific debate is over and is fond of reciting that "more than 2,600 scientists" have signed a letter supporting his view of "global climatic disruption." However, this too is not true. The vast majority of the signatories to Mr. Gore's letter are *not* scientists—they include lawyers, medical doctors, dentists, landscape architects, a philosopher and a diplomat. The fact is that 93% of the signatories have no expertise in climate studies.

It appears the unsavory truth was accidentally revealed by Richard Bendick, a Clinton-Gore State Department employee, who said: "A global climate treaty must be implemented even if there is no scientific evidence to back the greenhouse effect."

In today's technologically advanced society, the public is often required to trust in experts. All too often misrepresentation and manipulation have been the result. Nowhere is this more evident than in the Administration's stance on global warming and the Kyoto Protocol.

Enter Stephen Schneider who helps the Clinton-Gore team promote their climate change policy. Schneider appears to be a trustworthy expert: researcher at the National Center for Atmospheric Research, a professorship with Stanford's

Department of Biological Sciences and a Ph.D. in Plasma Physics from Columbia University.

However, appearances can be deceiving. On global warming, Schneider freely admits he casts scientific caution aside and ignores the direct evidence. He said, "Looking at every bump and wiggle of the record is a waste of time...So, I don't set very much store by looking at the direct evidence." Looking at the direct evidence is a waste of time? A stunning mind set for a scientist! In the world of Gore and Schneider, science is not driven by evidence, it is driven by raw politics.

Perhaps this explains why only two decades ago Schneider was not sounding the alarm on warming, but warned of an impending ice age. Schneider, who now warns of catastrophic global warming, was at the forefront of the global cooling hysteria in the 1970s. He published a book entitled *The Genesis Strategy*, warning of a coming glaciation. He wrote a testimonial for Lowell Ponte's *The Cooling*. Schneider also co-authored a paper on carbon dioxide and aerosols in which he argued that the impact of aerosols "is to reduce the surface temperature of Earth...[I]f sustained over a period of several years, such a temperature decrease over the whole globe is believed to be sufficient to trigger an ice age."

Additionally, Schneider harshly criticized the then-budding warming theory. In 1971, he wrote, "Temperatures do not increase in proportion to an atmospheric increase in carbon dioxide...Even an eight-fold increase...might warm the earth's surface less than two degrees [Celsius], and this is highly unlikely in the next several thousand years." In two decades, Schneider went from hysterical warnings of an impeding ice age to frenzied predictions of global warming—all the while paying little heed to the "direct evidence."

The commotion and hysteria of global warming is nothing new. Those with a political agenda concoct an emergency and propose onerous government regulations and higher taxes as the solution. These emergency mongers then ask us to pay the price for their "solution" in lost jobs and higher costs for everything from groceries, to fuel, to housing. They assure us that avoiding their contrived disaster will be worth the heavy price.

Beware! Amidst Gore's warnings of imminent climate doom, we must remember that many of the same "experts" that now preach the horrors of global warming not long ago warned of a new ice age. They can't have it both ways.

Governmental Price Gouging and Collusion

(Originally published in September 2000)

Less than eighteen months ago, motorists were cruising on gasoline prices of under $1 a gallon. Now prices have hit $1.65—even $2.00 or $2.50 in some cities—and motorists are understandably upset.

Never one to miss an opportunity to grandstand, Al Gore called on the Federal Trade Commission to open a formal inquiry into "possible collusion, illegal price gouging and outrageous profit taking" by his favorite villain, Big Oil.

Many people were more than a little puzzled by his heated rhetoric. This is the same Al Gore who has been advocating higher energy prices for years. When one of Gore's fondest wishes is coming true, why the crocodile tears?

Gore's 1992 book, *Earth in the Balance*, championed sharply higher taxes on fossil fuels as "one of the logical first steps" in saving the planet from "what is perhaps the single greatest threat to the environment"—the internal combustion engine.

In 1993, he cast the tie-breaking Senate vote to increase federal gasoline taxes by 4.3 cents a gallon—boosting combined state and federal gas taxes to as much as 80 cents a gallon. He continues to resist even a temporary reduction in the 18-cents-per-gallon federal excise tax on gasoline to offset price hikes caused by the complex maze of federal and state rules on reformulated gasoline.

Gore's adamant opposition to oil drilling in Alaska and off the U.S. coast means huge prospects cannot be explored even under strict environmental safeguards, and America remains dependent on pricey foreign oil. In stark contrast, he refuses to criticize drilling on environmentally sensitive ancestral Indian lands in Colombia by Occidental Petroleum, a company in which he owns at least $500,000 in stock.

Gore has been advocating that average Americans drive small, unsafe automobiles to reduce their energy consumption. But he is chauffeured around at our expense in huge, gas-guzzling cars. Additionally, Gore sings nothing but praise for Leonardo DeCaprio, who drives an SUV, rode in a limousine to the Earth Day 2000 events (to lecture us about environmental values) and loves flying to New York City to go shopping.

Now Mr. Gore wants to dispense $48 billion in tax credits to people who buy more fuel-efficient cars and homes. The new federal program would take money from average taxpayers, reward people wealthy enough to afford new homes and cars and hire more bureaucrats to run the new programs.

But all this is merely a warm-up for his warming crusade. In 1997, the Vice President and thousands of climate alarmists flew gas-guzzling, carbon dioxide-spewing jetliners to Kyoto, Japan—to promote a treaty that would require the United States to slash carbon dioxide (CO_2) emissions that they claim cause global warming. Why not pick-up the phone or teleconference instead?

Never mind that satellites and weather balloons have found virtually no discernible warming over the past twenty years, except in Alaska and Siberia at night in mid-winter. Never mind that even United Nations' climate models now predict the planet will warm by only 1.5°F by 2030—instead of by 5°F, as they projected in 1988.

Never mind that the National Center for Atmospheric Research has calculated that even "perfect compliance" with the Kyoto Protocol would reduce predicted global warming by only 0.05 degrees by 2050. And never mind that over 17,000 scientists have signed statements saying, "There is no compelling evidence that humans are causing discernible climate change."

Al Gore and his cohorts in the Environmental Protection Agency (EPA), extreme environmental groups and the UN believe fervently in global warming. Or at least they believe fervently that they have the wisdom to justly dictate our energy use and economic futures.

But meeting the Kyoto Protocol's emission requirements carries a hefty price tag. Over the first ten years of the Kyoto Protocol, participating countries will incur compliance costs well in excess of $5 trillion, says Canadian economist Ross McKitrick. Americans would have to reduce their carbon dioxide emissions by 7% below 1990 levels—which means slashing their expected use of fossil fuels by about 40% within the next decade.

According to the Energy Information Agency, gasoline prices would have to be increased by an additional fifty cents a gallon and electricity costs would have to be almost doubled, to "encourage" this level of energy conservation. Obviously, an 85% jump in their air conditioning bills would affect poor and elderly Americans much more than an average annual temperature rise of 0.05°F. Millions would be forced to choose between heat and food in the winter and to turn off their air conditioners during summer heat waves.

Complying with Kyoto would also mean America's gross domestic product would decline by about 4% a year, food costs would rise 9%, medical costs would rise by 11% and housing costs would soar by 20%, according to Dr. Margo

Thorning, lead economist for the American Council for Capital Formation. All that to reduce theoretical global warming by 0.05°F.

"If there's evidence of what I suspect there's evidence of, it ought to be dealt with swiftly and harshly," Gore recently said about gas prices. Finally, Al Gore and I are in agreement—only I suspect he and I differ on who the culprits are. He would blame oil companies and business. I would blame a different crowd.

The collusion among government bureaucrats and radical environmentalists must be rooted out. Law-abiding American consumers should never be subjected to price gouging or forced to keep constant watch over their wallets, cars, air conditioners, charcoal grills and lawn mowers in the name of questionable global warming theories. Higher gasoline prices are only the beginning of what extreme environmentalists have planned for America.

Energy and the National Interest

(Originally published in January 2002)

Sooner or later, the immense oil and gas reserves in the Arctic National Wildlife Refuge—more commonly known as ANWR—must be tapped.

The Republican Minority in the Senate says sooner, the Democrat Majority prefers never. Senators in both parties who promised hard-core environmentalists they'd designate the area wilderness now have a dilemma. Do they keep their word, or risk being voted out of office when energy emergencies arise, as they surely will with Middle East oil supplies becoming increasingly unstable?

The House of Representatives showed courage last August by authorizing billions of dollars for research on alternative energy development and energy efficiency in a comprehensive energy bill.

In addition to encouraging conservation, the bill opened federal lands to exploration—but with stringent environmental safeguards. While allowing exploration on Alaska's frigid coastal plain, the House action limited drilling to just 2,000 acres—a relative flyspeck in the 19.6 million-acre barren refuge that few Americans have seen or will ever see.

Since September 11th, Americans in several national polls agreed with the House's decision to move forward with drilling in ANWR because the facts clearly show that the positives far outweigh the negatives.

Americans who have followed the issue know that 88% of our energy comes from oil, gas and coal; and that no combination of conservation, technology or alternatives can come close to replacing those fossil fuels. They also know it takes years for research, testing, permitting, construction and distribution systems to come on-line—regardless of the energy source.

What they don't know—and neither do energy experts—is how to predict energy supply and demand for the future—especially during a war on terror that could produce an energy crisis similar to the Arab oil embargo of 1973–1974.

Failure to confront a potential crisis places us in an untenable position. Aside from meeting the needs of a growing population, it takes eight times more petroleum to fuel military operations than it did during World War II. As our victory over the Taliban shows, that increased consumption more than pays for itself by keeping American casualties to the barest minimum.

Weaning ourselves from foreign oil is a key factor in reviving our sluggish economy as well. Oil imports reached 60% this year—including 1.2 million barrels a day from Iraq. More than 20,000 foreign supertankers continually off-loaded oil at U.S. refineries. While the oil is pumped off the tankers, hundreds of thousands of dollars are transferred every minute to foreign economies while our economy remains buried in the hard times following the attacks of September 11th.

Congress's overall attempts to address energy policy have been halfhearted and shortsighted thus far. We've had several national energy policies in the quarter-century since the Arab oil embargo, but they've focused on developing other nation's resources—not ours.

Since 1990, federal actions have removed more than 100 million acres of land from exploration. At the same time, not a single acre has been earmarked for increasing supply. Although America has abundant untapped oil reserves, mostly on federal lands, there have been no major discoveries—except in Alaska—in thirty years.

As a result, the petroleum industry lost more than 450,000 high-paying jobs in the 1990s and much of its infrastructure and expert workforce was dismantled. Last winter, when energy prices skyrocketed, the complacent politicians who encouraged the dismantling were outraged and demanded action. There was nothing industry or government could do at that point. Only unseasonably warm weather and a cutback in travel spurred by a recession and the trauma of September 11th saved us from a full-scale emergency.

We'd like to think the potential for an energy crisis no longer exists because prices and demand are down. Yet most senators admit, when pressed, that we need to find more oil and gas. The rub comes with the question, but where?

"Well, not in my state." If not onshore, how about offshore? Not off the East Coast. Certainly not off the West Coast. And there's little interest in the Gulf Coast.

Only Alaska wholeheartedly welcomes oil and gas development. In a state where a new survey reports more than 75% of respondents said they lived in Alaska because of its pristine environment, the same percentage supports ANWR development.

ANWR's petroleum resources are truly a national resource that should be shared with people in every state. Prohibiting drilling in this promising spot of land is a luxury we can't afford.

Environmentalists can end this stalemate. They should finally put energy, jobs and national security before preserving 2,000 acres of land set aside for energy production more than 25 years ago. America needs ANWR's oil and natural gas—sooner rather than later.

Enron & Global Warming: Putting Things into Perspective

(Originally published in February 2002)

Enron, the once powerful energy-trading corporation, is mired in financial ruin and scandal. Thousands of employees lost not only their jobs, but also their retirement accounts, which were invested almost entirely in now worthless Enron stock. Others whose retirement accounts held stock in the once robust Fortune 10 Company are also among those hit hard by the collapse. On Capitol Hill, it seems that just about everyone is scheduling hearings. Much of the nation and all of Washington, D.C. are agog that as much as $6 billion was lost.

All of this sounds pretty serious, but the reality is that the economic devastation could have been a lot worse. Here's how. A number of energy companies, including Enron, were strong supporters of the Kyoto Protocol (a.k.a. Global Warming Treaty) and international emissions trading. Enron and others believed that they would profit handsomely from the Clinton-Gore Administration's infatuation with the Kyoto treaty's command and control regulatory regime.

Enron envisioned itself as being a key player in the new international trading system. It would make a percentage of every trade it transacted. Additionally, since the Kyoto Protocol would reduce and eventually close down coal-fired power plants and encourage the use of gas-fired plants, Enron saw another chance to profit since much of its business was in natural gas.

In 1997, the U.S. Senate unanimously voted to advise the Clinton-Gore administration that it should not enter into any agreement to ration energy or harm the U.S. economy. It is extraordinarily rare that everyone in the Senate agrees on something. How often do Tom Daschle, Ted Kennedy, Jesse Helms and Trent Lott all agree?

That same year Enron officials met with Clinton and Gore at the White House to promote the Kyoto Protocol and emissions trading.

When the negotiations on the global warming treaty were breaking down and it appeared as if no agreement would be reached, Al Gore flew to Japan to personally accede to whatever unreasonable demands were made. The terms he agreed to were worse than most had ever imagined. However, Enron and others who hoped to benefit from this new regulatory scheme were pleased. In fact, an Enron internal memo boasted that the Kyoto Protocol would "do more to promote Enron's business than almost any other regulatory initiative..."

Unfortunately, we live in an era in which many businesses hope to succeed not by producing better products or by being more efficient, but by getting government to impose special interest regulations designed to give them an advantage in the marketplace. The problem with this approach is that someone has to pay the cost. In the case of the Kyoto Protocol, the cost was to be imposed on every American. We would have to pay more for everything from groceries, to fuel, to clothing, to heating and cooling.

If the Kyoto Protocol were ratified and in full force, experts estimate that Americans could lose between $100 billion and $400 billion—each year. Additionally, between 1 and 3.5 million jobs could be lost. That means that each household could lose an average of up to $6,000 each year. That is a lot to ask of Americans so that large energy companies could profit from this regulatory scheme. Moreover, a cost of $400 billion annually makes Enron's current one-time loss of $6 billion look like pocket change.

The point is not to minimize the difficulty and economic pain that Enron's failure has caused—but to highlight that if a one-time loss of $6 billion is worth worrying about, we should be that much more concerned about a loss of $400 billion each year. For the time being, we have avoided these catastrophic costs because the Clinton-Gore Administration was not successful in shoving the Global Warming Treaty down our throats.

We should thank President Bush for steadfastly standing up to the special interests that promoted the Kyoto Treaty. Despite the wishes of those powerful few that hoped to profit from the new regulatory mandates of Kyoto, President Bush did not cave-in. Instead, Bush sided with hardworking Americans who simply could not afford to foot the bill so that a few special interests could profit handsomely.

There are others who continue to push the Kyoto Protocol and energy rationing schemes. They would like to run roughshod over President Bush, take our jobs and pick our pockets. Beware. If they succeed, our economic pain will be a great deal more profound than anything experienced because of Enron's current financial collapse.

Chicken Little Saga: Temperature Fluctuation Doesn't Mean the Sky is Falling

(Originally published in April 2002)

For more than a decade, some politicians seeking more regulatory and taxing power have been telling us that the world's climate is warming. In this modern Chicken Little saga, we are not told that the sky is falling—instead, we are told that the climate is warming. Politicians have been telling us that our cars, homes and factories are causing the world's temperature to rise. They've never had a shred of sound scientific evidence for such claims. But when there are higher taxes to justify and heavier regulatory burdens to explain, it is best to have a catastrophe as the excuse.

These same politicians, wanting to give the impression of scientific support for their Chicken Little theory, gave away millions of our tax dollars to scientists who would push the global warming agenda. However, a researcher with a government grant saying human activity may be causing global warming is not science. Science is about evidence and facts, not opinions.

To bolster their weak scientific position, some researchers have created computer models that "predict" global warming. However, these same computer models have been "predicting" long-term climate trends incorrectly for decades. A computer predicts whatever the data and the software tell it to predict. For this reason, computer predictions are not scientific evidence.

Some in the media, seeking headlines that sell, have been complicit in this modern Chicken Little story. Every time there is a record-breaking temperature somewhere in the world, they report it as if it is news worthy. The fact is somewhere it will always be hotter than normal. It will also be cooler than normal somewhere. There is simply no statistical significance to a record-breaking day anywhere in the world.

Why do some politicians, researchers dependent on federal grant money and the press avoid real science when dealing with climate issues? Because real science does not support their Chicken Little theory.

Sound science shows that the world's climate has always fluctuated. Much of the earth was once covered in ice. Today most of the world is not. Those changes took place long before man invented cars, built heated and air-conditioned homes or constructed large factories.

For example, *The New York Times* recently reported that a study of tree rings shows that 1,000 years ago, global temperatures rose and led to a period of unusual warmth. Between 900 and 1100 A.D. Europe enjoyed a period of unusual warmth. The period is known as the Medieval Warm Period.

Researchers from Lamont-Doherty Earth Observatory and the Swiss Federal Research Institute took tree samples from Louisiana to Alaska and found that a similar warm period occurred in North America. No one blames warming that occurred 1,000 years ago on man or his inventions. Most scientists agree that variations in the sun's intensity caused the climate changes in the past.

But today, even when modest fluctuations in temperature occur, we are told—without scientific evidence—that humans or human activities are causing the warming. Environmentalists and some in the media have made much of the melting of the Larsen B ice shelf in Antarctica. They argue that the melting ice is evidence of human-induced global warming. To the casual observer, this may pass for sound science. But it is not.

The ice caps once covered much of the world. They've been melting for a long time—not quite as long as the Sun has been rising in the East, but almost that long. The sun rising and ice melting are not news.

But don't take my word for it—glaciologists agree that Antarctica is not suffering from a warming trend. In fact, many parts of Antarctica are growing colder, not warmer. For example, the West Antarctic Ice Sheet and the ice sheet on the Ross Sea are growing larger and thicker, not melting. Researchers at the University of Illinois report that there has been a "net cooling on the Antarctic continent between 1966 and 2000." In some regions the cooling was significant—up to two degrees centigrade per decade.

The bottom line is simple. There is one constant in temperature and climate—things change. Climate has been changing since the world began. It will continue to change and fluctuate. You can bank on it. Natural change and fluctuation is not evidence that the sky is falling.

An Energy Bill that Only Saddam Hussein Could Love

(Originally published in May 2002)

A year ago, the White House released a comprehensive energy plan to make America more energy independent and secure. It included conservation and more production. A few months later, the House passed an energy bill that was compatible with the president's plan. Under the heavy hand of Majority Leader Tom Daschle (D-SD), the Senate recently passed a very different kind of energy bill. The Senate bill would force America's continued dependence on foreign oil, raise energy prices for consumers and grow the federal government at the expense of taxpayers.

Shortly, the House and Senate will impanel a conference committee to hammer out the differences between their two energy bills. The question is, what will emerge from this conference committee? Will it be an energy bill that makes America stronger and more independent? Or will it be an anti-energy bill that weakens America and empowers the likes of Saddam Hussein? No one knows for sure what the final bill will look like, but if Senators Daschle, John Kerry (D-Mass.) and Joe Lieberman (D-Conn.) get their way, Saddam Hussein will soon be smiling broadly.

Last year, we produced 40 % less oil in the United States than we did in 1970 because over the years environmental regulations have made it increasingly difficult to explore and drill for oil in the United States. Senate Democrats worked overtime to make sure that America will not drill for more of its own oil, but instead will continue its reliance on Middle Eastern oil. Absent productive action, our dependence on foreign oil will only worsen. Saddam is smiling.

We must either produce more of our own energy or allow the likes of Saddam Hussein to hold us hostage with his oil. Apparently, Senators Daschle, Kerry and Lieberman have determined that it would be better to send American men and women to fight and die in the Middle East than to even consider drilling on 2000 acres of frozen tundra in Alaska. But they did not stop there.

The Senate's anti-energy bill would also usher in through the backdoor the crippling regulatory regime of the Kyoto global warming treaty. This is the same treaty that the U.S. Senate opposed 95-to-0 only a few years ago on grounds that it would kill American jobs, dig into the pocketbooks and wallets of Americans and unfairly shackle the American economy. Defenders of the bill argue that the requirements of the bill are "voluntary." However, the bill expressly provides that the regulatory requirements will be mandatory in five years unless people voluntarily comply. In other words, you must "voluntarily" comply or they will require you by law to comply. This turns voluntary on its head.

The Senate bill would require everyone from automakers to soda bottlers and brewers to report to the federal government both direct and indirect "emissions" from their products. I don't mean to be difficult, but how is America benefited and how are our energy woes improved because A&W Root Beer is forced to report to the government how much carbonation (or CO_2) is released when a can of their soda is opened? Mr. Daschle, Saddam is smiling.

The Senate bill also includes a "renewable portfolio standard" that requires utilities to produce 10% of their electricity from non-hydro renewable sources by 2019. This means that in coming years, every American will pay more for electricity. If you doubt that energy will cost more, ask yourself if the new requirements actually produce energy more affordably, why is a federal mandate required to force their use? Wouldn't even the greediest company use these "renewable" sources if they produced affordable electricity? And if these mandates produce an abundance of affordable energy, why require only 10%? The answer is simple—this "renewable portfolio standard" will cost consumers billions and do virtually nothing to increase energy production. Take notice that Saddam is smiling.

Let's speak plainly and clearly. The Senate's anti-energy bill is bad for America's security and our economy. It is a bill that only Saddam Hussein could love. Whether Saddam has continued reason to smile will depend on what happens in the conference committee and what the final energy bill looks like. But, alas, Senator Daschle is off to a bad start. Instead of assigning Senators from his party with real expertise in energy to serve on the conference committee, he has assigned a group of his partisan allies who appear ready to push the Senate's anti-energy bill. Saddam is smiling, Mr. Daschle, and America is watching.

Energy: *National Security, the Economy, and the Environment*

(Originally published in December 2002)

The lame duck session in Congress has ended. In January, a new Congress will convene. One of the most important and contentious debates of 2003 will focus on energy. Energy dominated much of 2002 debate. But, in the end, Congress could not agree. So the energy debate will continue into 2003. The stakes will be high because energy affects national security, the economy and environmental sensibilities.

America imports almost 60% of its oil—mostly from the Middle East. America is prosecuting a war against terrorism, which has deep roots in the Middle East. It is rather obvious that America will be more secure if it can produce more of its own oil. If we allow our enemies to hold us hostage with oil, we do so at our own peril. Yet, in 2002, liberals in the U.S. Senate led the charge to prevent oil exploration in Alaska's Arctic National Wildlife Refuge (ANWR). They ensured that America will continue to grow ever more dependent upon folks like Saddam Hussein for oil.

Energy is the fuel of our economy. For our economy to regain its strength and maintain stable growth, we must have affordable, plentiful and stable energy. Policies that make energy more expensive, less stable or more scarce will stunt the economy, will kill jobs and hit our pocketbooks. Yet, Senate liberals pushed policies designed to make energy more scare and expensive—mandates for windmills that don't work, less domestic oil production and more "voluntary" government regulation of carbon dioxide (CO_2), a harmless gas that humans breath out and plants require to sustain life.

For the sake of our national security and economic well-being, we must increase domestic oil production, develop alternative energy sources and reduce our dependence on unstable foreign oil. Extreme environmentalists claim that oil exploration will destroy the environment and cannot produce enough oil to help. They are wrong on both counts.

In the 1970s, President Carter and the Democratically controlled Congress created ANWR and set aside a small part of ANWR specifically for oil and gas exploration. Bush has proposed exploration in this specifically set aside area—precisely as Carter and Congress intended.

ANWR is the size of South Carolina or about twenty million acres—which is about 5% of the land in Alaska. The proposed drilling site in ANWR is less than 2000 acres—which is less than 1/100 of 1% of ANWR. Denver's airport is 17 times larger than the proposed drilling site in ANWR. If Alaska were a football field, the ANWR drilling site would be smaller than a postage stamp. If Alaska were a two-hour movie, the drilling site would be less than the blink of an eye—only four one-hundredths of a second. Such small scale drilling cannot possibly destroy the environment—particularly given the new technologies employed to safeguard the environment.

Years ago when energy production in nearby Prudhoe Bay was debated, similar environmental scare-tactics were employed. But, during a quarter-century of intensive energy production, there has been a 400% increase to the caribou herd and the environment is clean and beautiful.

Experts estimate that ANWR contains up to 16 billion barrels of oil. It would take the United States thirty years at our current import levels to buy that much oil from Saudi Arabia. Drilling in ANWR would be a strong first step to America becoming more energy independent. It would also show our enemies that we will not be held hostage by oil.

During the upcoming energy debate, environmental scare-tactics will again be thrown about. But, America must deal in facts. And in a post-September 11th world, we must decide if we are content to give hostile powers the means to hold us hostage.

SUVs, Terrorists and Fertile Imaginations

(Originally published in January 2003)

The connection between the drug trade and terrorism has been established by years of experience and hard evidence. Terrorists, whose life mission is to kill as many Americans as possible, not surprisingly deal in illegal drugs to fund their work of terror, destruction and death. Thus, the Administration has created ads pointing out that those who buy illegal drugs are funding our enemies' mayhem.

Recently, Arrianna Huffington and a handful of Hollywood elites decided to create television ads that assert that driving Sport Utility Vehicles (SUVs) also funds terrorism. In their confused minds, driving an SUV is as bad as buying cocaine. In fact, the ads state that by driving SUVs, Americans "helped hijack an airplane" and gave "money to a terrorist training camp."

Ms. Huffington and her Hollywood friends need to get their facts straight. A course in logical reasoning would help, too. First, there is not an ounce of evidence that driving larger automobiles or driving longer distances helps fund terrorism. Osama bin Laden does not own an oil well or oil company. Terrorists don't sell oil. Terrorists don't make a cut from our oil purchases.

Second, it is simple-minded thinking to argue that since we buy some of our oil from the Middle East, and many terrorists have ties to the same region, that buying oil gives terrorists money. If this line of reasoning had any rationality, those who drink coffee could be said to support and promote the sale of cocaine to America's children. After all, a lot of our coffee comes from Columbia and cocaine drug cartels also are located there. Of course, this is absurd and nonsensical. But if we apply Ms. Huffington's confused brand of logic, then everyone who drinks coffee at Starbucks is giving aid to drug kingpins and promoting the sale of cocaine to children. Perhaps this will be Ms. Huffington's next crusade.

These ads are so factually flawed that many television stations have refused to air them and thus lost the advertising revenues. One ABC affiliate director of programming in New York said, "There were a lot of statements being made that were not backed up…" That is the polite way to say, "Ms. Huffington is fabricating this whole thing."

So what is really going on here? Ms. Huffington and her Hollywood elite friends don't trust you and me to choose the right car for ourselves and they don't trust the competitive marketplace to encourage carmakers to design more fuel-efficient cars. So they want federal regulators to have the power to force you and me to purchase smaller, less safe cars and to require manufactures to make cars that you and I don't want to buy.

They do not believe that we buy cars that meet the needs of our families and businesses. They also do not understand that carmakers make what we want to buy. Carmakers would love to be able to advertise that their SUVs and mini vans are more powerful, more comfortable and go twice as far on a gallon of gas. Thus, they are motivated to make improvements as technology and costs permit. For example, GM recently announced a new lineup of innovative hybrid-powered trucks and SUVs. The government did not make them do it. They did it in hopes that lower fuel costs will attract more buyers. Competition, not government regulation, drives advances.

That societal elites don't trust the common man and woman is nothing new, but it is shocking that they would falsely claim that Americans who drive SUVs and mini vans "helped hijack an airplane." Shame on Ms. Huffington for misusing the tragic events of September 11th as a publicity stunt. She owes America an apology.

Global Warming Enthusiasts: Wrong on the Science and Indifferent to the Poor

(Originally published in July 2003)

During most of the last twelve years, those with a political ax to grind told us that global warming was "for real," the evidence was "in," and the debate was "over." They repeated this line often enough that many folks began to believe it. However, unrelenting repetition of an inaccuracy does not make it true.

So what evidence do adherents of global warming dogma rely upon? They don't rely on historical temperature records—which show that climate has always fluctuated and that there has been no significant warming trend over the last fifty years. They don't rely on NASA satellite data or weather balloon data which also show that there is no noteworthy warming. They don't rely upon polar ice cap data because the ice caps are growing thicker in some places and thinner in others.

So what do global warming enthusiasts rely upon? Computer models—ones that do not work. These computer models cannot accurately "back-predict" the climate trends of the last 100 years. If we input the data from the last century, the computer model—if it worked—would accurately "predict" current global climate conditions. But they cannot. These models produce wildly different and spectacularly incorrect results. In fact, environmental scientists at the University of Virginia reviewed and tested these computer models and found that they produced no better results than a table of randomly selected numbers applied to climate data.

If the climate models can't do any better than a roll of the dice, should we rely on them? Should we base costly public policy on a crapshoot? Should regulatory schemes based on these faulty numbers force Americans to pay more to heat and cool their homes, feed and clothe their families and drive to and from work and school?

This brings me to my second point. Global warming enthusiasts apparently don't care about the poor. This may sound harsh, but facts speak loudly. Millionaires may not care if their monthly heating bill increases by $185 or their grocery bill increases by $115. They can afford it. But the poor cannot.

During a harsh winter, should public policy based on the roll of a dice force poor seniors or single mothers with small children to choose between heating and eating? These questions are particularly troubling when the regulations that would force these cruel choices on the poor are based on junk science and chance numbers.

These are real-life issues, not silly hypotheticals. Recently, Senator Jim Jeffords (I-Vt.), Chairman of the Environment and Public Works Committee, held hearings on a bill, S.B. 556, that would implement much of the regulatory scheme envisioned by global warming enthusiasts. The committee invited J. Thomas Mullen who leads Catholic Charities in Cleveland, Ohio to testify about the impact on the poor of the proposed bill. Mr. Mullen's organization serves over 600,000 needy children and families, senior citizens, persons with disabilities and homeless persons.

Mr. Mullen testified that a recent study "reported that one-quarter of Americans [have] problems paying for several basic necessities. [C]urrently 23% have difficulty in paying their utilities—that is, one out of four Americans." Mr. Mullen went on to say that if the global warming regulatory agenda were implemented, "we could see the difficulty in Cleveland reach beyond one out of two people and families not able to pay utilities…"

Mr. Mullen emphasized that two groups are most vulnerable. First, is the elderly. "[A]pproximately one half (49.4%) of persons over 65 years old [in Cleveland] have incomes less that $15,000 per year…The second group that…will be hurt similarly by this is children. In Cleveland, over one-fourth of all children live in poverty and are in a family of a single female head of household. These children will suffer further loss of basic needs as their moms are forced to make choices of whether to pay the rent or live in a shelter; pay the heating bill or…buy food…These are not choices any senior citizen, child, or, for that matter, person in America should make."

Yet, these are precisely the sorts of decisions that global warming enthusiasts are attempting to force on the poor. Lousy science and indifference to the poor—that is the legacy of global warming adherents.

Mr. Mullen concluded, "I ask the [Senate] to look carefully at the ramifications of [the global warming regulatory agenda] and its impact on employment and energy costs. We have many vulnerable people…across America who cannot carry the burden of this legislation." Well said Mr. Mullen. Let's hope the Senate was listening.

Energy, Trial Lawyers & Extortion

(Originally published in February 2004)

Last year in the Senate, the Energy bill stalled, primarily due to a common-sense provision, which would rein in the out-of-control elements of the trial bar and protect manufacturers of Methyl Tertiary Butyl Ether (MTBE) from outrageous efforts by trial attorneys to score a big payday. So far this year, that same provision appears to be a major roadblock to passage of the Energy Bill.

Legislators need to understand that, contrary to the screaming and inaccurate rhetoric from those who want the provision removed, the provision does not protect ANY industry, company or individual who actually bears responsibility for leaking materials that pollute our waterways. It WILL, however, protect innocent parties and industries (such as MTBE manufacturers) from complete destruction at the hands of trial lawyer lies.

Don't just take my word for it—take a look at what's happening out there in the real world.

Several weeks ago, officials from the City of Santa Monica, California announced to great fanfare an incredibly large settlement in a lawsuit over city drinking water wells contaminated by the gasoline additive MTBE. The settlement calls for several oil companies to build and pay for a water treatment facility that will clean up the pollution, and to pay the city close to $100 million. Trial lawyer greed is now threatening to derail this settlement and delay the restoration of the city's drinking water.

In the words of Santa Monica Mayor Richard Bloom, the settlement was a "landmark achievement" and, according to Bloom, the city will now "reclaim its water supply." In fact, at first glance, this settlement looks like a textbook example of how the legal system is supposed to work. The city wells were polluted by gasoline leaks at nearby service stations. The city sued. The parties responsible for the pollution were identified and agreed to pay the cleanup costs and penalties.

But the story doesn't stop there. What the city swept under the rug when it announced the settlement was that it was proceeding with the lawsuit against one remaining defendant that has not settled the case. Lyondell Chemical Company was added as a defendant in the suit as an afterthought, ten years after the case was filed. According to the city's trial lawyers, Lyondell should pay big bucks because Lyondell sold MTBE to refiners who blended it with gasoline and then sold it to gas stations—some of whom stored the fuel in leaky underground tanks that seeped into the groundwater.

So a company that had nothing to do with the transportation and storage of the gasoline is being sued for the impact of someone else's gasoline leaking out of someone else's underground storage tanks.

With that reason, it is miraculous that Microsoft has escaped being named in the suit because its Windows operating system was most likely used in drafting and emailing the agreements that documented the original sale of MTBE. Trial lawyers are nothing, if not wildly creative.

To its credit, Lyondell Chemical Company is holding its ground. It recently filed a motion contesting the settlement unless the City of Santa Monica and the trial lawyers pulling the city's strings dropped their absurd claim against Lyondell.

Ask yourself, who benefits from proceeding with the case now that those responsible for the pollution have agreed to shell out money for groundwater restoration and penalties? Not the city or its residents—this will only hold up approval of the settlement and stall environmental cleanup efforts. Certainly not Lyondell Chemical Company which had nothing to do with the Santa Monica pollution to begin with. The only ones who stand to gain are the greedy trial lawyers who, even though the case has been favorably resolved, want more money for themselves.

Make no mistake, for trial lawyers, MTBE is the new cause du jour. To them, MTBE is an acronym that stands for "Money To Be Extorted."

With a little luck and common sense in Washington, trial attorneys will no longer have the ability to pull this kind of trick, and will need to focus their energies where they belong—on going after parties that are actually guilty of something. The Bush administration's plan is to put an end to the kind of nonsense we've been forced to watch in Santa Monica. Let's hope those in Congress have enough courage to pass this common sense reform.

Global Warming: From Bipartisan to Partisan

(Originally published in March 2004)

My, how things can change! In 1997, the Senate voted 95-to-0 for the Byrd-Hagel Resolution which stated that "it is the sense of the Senate that...the United States should not be a signatory to [the Kyoto Global Warming Treaty]." Ninety-five Senators voted in favor of this resolution. Zero opposed it. That means that every single Republican and Democrat who voted, voted for the resolution condemning the Kyoto Global Warming Treaty. That's not just bipartisan, that's unanimous!

It is nearly impossible to get a unanimous vote in the Senate. The fact that a unanimous Senate had such serious reservations about Kyoto Global Warming Treaty says something.

Since President George W. Bush took office over three years ago, he has been constantly attacked and excoriated by radical greens as being anti-environment. Even ABC News and John Stossell ran a special news report about how the radical greens are trying to brainwash school children into believing that Bush is reflexively anti-environment.

Often the president's detractors have centered their criticisms around his position on the Kyoto Global Warming Treaty—which happens to be very close to the 95-to-0 position of the U.S. Senate. John Kerry has even argued that if he would agree to Kyoto's terms, the French and Germans would have supported us in Iraq. This is so absurd that it is beneath the dignity of a man who would like to be president.

To listen to eco-radicals tell the story, it is a proven scientific fact that the climate is warming and that mankind is to blame. Moreover, they accuse Bush of being irresponsible and virtually alone in his stand against the Kyoto Global Warming Treaty.

Yet, nothing could be farther from the truth. President Bush is simply acknowledging what the responsible scientific community has been saying for some time—the scientific evidence behind the global warming theory is weak. Bush is standing with the 95 Senators who voted not to sign the Kyoto Global Warming Treaty unless its many shortcomings were adequately resolved.

It is the leftist greens who stand with the ZERO Senators who voted against the resolution. If the leftist greens couldn't find even ONE Senator—Republican or Democrat—to cast a vote in their direction, what does that tell you about the leftist greens' position? So who is out of the mainstream? Who is extreme? Whose position flies in the face of science, sound public policy and common sense? It isn't the 95 Senators and it isn't President Bush.

Here are the facts. First, the earth's temperature naturally fluctuates. Ice once covered much of North America. Fortunately, warmer weather melted that ice and made the land habitable. Second, roughly 80% of the carbon dioxide (CO_2) which radical greens complain causes warming was emitted after 1940. Yet, most of the 0.5° C "warming" they blame on carbon dioxide emissions occurred between 1850 and 1940—after several centuries of cooling known as the Little Ice Age. If the one-half degree warming occurred before the carbon dioxide was emitted, then the carbon dioxide could not have caused the warming. You don't have to be a scientist to understand that a cause-effect relationship implies a sequence—first the cause, then the effect.

President Bush is not a scientist, but he understands that the great weight of current scientific evidence does not support the eco-radical's global warming agenda. He also understands that signing a treaty that has little chance of improving the environment and that will dramatically reduce the supply of energy and increase its cost is not in our best interest. Finally, he understands that agreeing with a unanimous U.S. Senate and literally thousands of scientists does not make his position extreme or fringe. It is time for the real extremists to face and accept these facts.

Talking the Talk, But Skipping the Walk

(Originally published in April 2004)

Talk is cheap and nowhere is this more true than listening to our European counterparts whine and complain that the United States is not sufficiently supportive of the United Nations' global warming treaty known as the Kyoto Protocol. John Kerry has absurdly argued that if George Bush had been more supportive of the Kyoto Protocol, then France and Germany would have been willing to support us in Iraq.

Other nations talk about the importance of the Kyoto Protocol and have recently taken to sanctimonious preaching aimed at the United States and the Bush administration for not ratifying the Protocol. However, they don't mean it and we shouldn't take them seriously. Here's why—they may talk as if they support the Kyoto Protocol, but their actions belie their words. Simply stated, we must pay less heed to their words and more attention to their actions. They talk one way and act another. Actions speak louder than words.

With the United States standing as essentially the sole voice against the insanity of the Kyoto Protocol, some extreme environmentalists are asking, "If the rest of the world supports the Kyoto Protocol, why can't the United States?" This question sounds a great deal more relevant than it actually is.

The better question would be, if the rest of the world is so excited about the Kyoto Protocol, why don't they do more than just posture and talk? Why don't they do something? Why don't their actions match their words? Virtually no European nations have ratified the Kyoto Protocol. They talk, but do nothing. Yet, despite their own reluctance to support the Protocol, they complain that the United States needs to be more supportive.

So why do the Europeans and most of the rest of the world talk out of one side of their mouth and then act in a completely contrary way? The answer is two fold.

For some nations, the Kyoto Protocol is a chance to hamstring the U.S. economy and thereby make themselves more competitive. Nations such as China, India and Brazil would not be burdened by the Protocol and thus view it as a great opportunity to slow down our economic strength so that they can overtake the United States and other developed economies.

For other nations, the Kyoto Protocol is the perfect chance to politically placate extreme eco-radicals, while avoiding the economic havoc that the Protocol

would bring to their nations. Simply stated, they get to be on record as supporting the Protocol, but they don't have to live with its heavy costs or the economic
destruction it would wreak because they know that the Bush Administration will
not succumb to their foolish and empty rhetoric. They get a free ride on Bush's
courage and leadership.

The Kyoto Protocol will do virtually nothing to reduce carbon dioxide (CO_2)
in the atmosphere. Even its supporters now acknowledge that without the partic-
ipation of China, India, Brazil and other developing nations, the Protocol cannot
accomplish its stated objectives.

For the record, carbon dioxide is a harmless, naturally occurring gas and has
been part of the air mankind has been breathing since the beginning of time. In
fact, without carbon dioxide, life could not be sustained on Earth.

The only thing the Protocol would successfully do to the United States and
other economic powers is hamstring their economic growth and impose significant cost increases on consumers for everything from fuel, to electricity, to groceries. This is why foreign leaders talk big, but don't act. They want to have it
both ways.

While they won't admit it, European leaders inwardly cheer when Bush points
out the Protocol's many fatal flaws. But publicly, they whine that the United
States needs to push the Protocol forward. The fact is they couldn't be happier
that the Bush administration is questioning the Protocol's basic assumptions, its
necessity, its impact and its cost. His doing the right thing gives them the luxury
of political pandering.

So next time some politician launches into a Kyoto Protocol "sermon" and
criticizes the United States or President Bush for not ratifying the misguided
treaty, ask why they haven't ratified the treaty. Ask why they haven't done anything to push for the Protocol's passage. Ask why, for the past decade, all they've
done is utter words, but never done a thing.

Action speaks louder than words. And talk is cheap.

Entertainment or Propaganda?

(Originally published in June 2004)

As only Hollywood and its multimillion-dollar special effects can, the movie *The Day After Tomorrow* depicts floods, tidal waves, hurricanes and other extreme weather events as the result of human-caused global climate change. Perhaps this is just more fun and fictional entertainment from Hollywood. Who would criticize the *Lord of the Rings* movies for being unrealistic? Wasn't that part of the show? But extreme global warming adherents are excited for the release of *The Day After Tomorrow* because they hope Americans will view it as an accurate depiction of science.

Perhaps they are right, but I doubt it. I don't think Americans view movies such as *Jurassic Park* or *Armageddon* as serious efforts at scientific inquiry. They were fun movies, but they were not sound science. Likewise, *The Day After Tomorrow* may be fun entertainment, but it is not science.

Unfortunately, there will be some who attempt to use this Hollywood special effects extravaganza as proof that man is causing global warming and that extreme energy taxes and regulations must be adopted immediately to save us from the horrors depicted in the movie. This is as silly as basing America's energy, environmental and economic policy on children's cartoon movies like *Ice Age* or *Lion King*.

One of the favorite ploys of extreme environmentalists is to use politically motivated pseudo-science in an attempt to scare Americans into accepting their job-killing environmental policies and burdensome regulatory regimes. They conjure up some urgent and terrible risk to the environment and our health. Then they promise us that if we will give them the power to regulate the economy, kill jobs and increase prices for basic goods and services, they will rescue us from the catastrophe that they have predicted.

The problem is their claims of future catastrophes are based on shoddy junk science. Their claims are not true or real. But the economic devastation that they cause is real. The jobs lost are also real. The increased costs for energy, food, goods and services are real.

Extreme environmentalists claim that the climate is warming and that it is man's fault. They tell us the debate is over and that the science is certain. John Kerry parrots this line and has used his power in the U.S. Senate to support job-killing regulations, higher energy prices and greater U.S. dependence on foreign oil. Kerry has also worked to make it harder for Americans to drive the cars they need and want for business and their family—all of this while promising that if elected, he would make jobs a priority. It sounds like junk science would be his priority, not jobs.

There is no reliable scientific data proving man is causing global climate change or that such modest changes, if they were to occur, would cause any real harm. The one constant on earth is that climate has always changed. We have had ice ages and warmer periods and mini-ice ages—many times. None of this is new.

The world's current temperature averages are cooler than the average for the last 10,000 years. Yet despite this fact, we are promised by warming adherents that if we allow them to restrict and tax energy and kill jobs, they will save us from warmer temperatures. Even if one accepts their premise, the solutions they offer will not solve the problem they claim exists. Their claims of man-made climate change are just so much hot air. Unfortunately, the jobs they would kill are real and the poverty they would inflict on Americans is real—all this to fix an imaginary problem.

Americans should not trust Hollywood movies or extreme environmentalists as reliable sources for sound scientific data. Nor should Americans take seriously their political demands for more taxes and job-killing regulations.

3

Economic Liberty and Property Rights

Keeping More of Your Own Money is Bad for America?

(Originally published in September 2003)

Years ago, I was in a debate with a sitting member of Congress who sat on the Ways and Means Committee. In defending his opposition to tax cuts, he concluded by saying, "We can't afford tax cuts." When my turn came, I said to the audience, "I can afford a tax cut. Can you afford a tax cut?" The audience went wild with applause and made it clear they could afford a tax cut. I continued, "Did you notice when he said, 'We can't afford a tax cut,' he didn't mean you and me—the taxpayers. He meant the government. He thinks he represents the government, not us."

This is typical of liberals. Their love of big government causes them to be more concerned about funding government programs than allowing families to fund their own needs. For example, if families can keep more of their own income, they can buy their first home, save for their children's college tuition, pay for their children's piano or dance lessons, pay for a family vacation or save for retirement—to name only a few.

In the debate, I explained that I supported tax cuts because I was confident that families would spend the money better than big government would. Moreover, it is THEIR money. Why do liberals believe they have a right to the property of others? Why do they believe that they spend our money better than we can?

I realize it is axiomatic that as citizens of a free nation, we have an obligation to pay our fair share to fund the necessary and legitimate costs of a frugal government. However, the federal government spends well beyond this basic level of necessary spending. It spends more than $21,000 per household. Simply stated, the government does not have the right to spend money like a drunken sailor and then hand the bill to working families, demanding that it be paid as a matter of good citizenship.

The premise of President Bush's recent tax cut and jobs growth package is that when families have more of their own money to spend, families are better off and the economy will grow. It is surprising how vehement liberals and some of the dominant media culture have been in arguing against the tax cuts.

Liberals evidently believe that families and individuals are benefited by paying a lot of taxes and hoping the government will then fund things that the family and individual would have wanted in the first place. When given a choice between funding government programs and allowing people to keep more of their own money to fund their own dreams and aspirations, liberals clearly prefer to fund government.

Let's examine some of the arguments that often surface whenever tax cuts are discussed and see which ones stand up to scrutiny and which ones are merely rhetorical devices.

What do lower tax rates have to do with a strong economy?

First, taxing things discourages the behavior that is taxed. For example, every time another increase in the cigarette tax is proposed, we are told that it will discourage people from smoking. What then are we left to believe that high income tax rates will discourage? The answer—work and productivity. Do we really want a policy that discourages and punishes hard work, productivity and entrepreneurship? Liberals do.

The fact is high tax rates are a price imposed by government on productive behavior—as a result, people will work less, invest less, be less productive and be less entrepreneurial. An economy where fewer people are working, where there is declining investment and productivity and where entrepreneurship is slipping is an economy in decline—either in a recession or depression.

Low tax rates do the opposite—reward and encourage work, investment, productivity and entrepreneurship. This stimulates economic and job growth because the taxes on additional economic output is lowered. Some folks think that tax cuts "pump" more money into the economy, but this is not the real benefit. The real benefit is that productive behavior is encouraged and rewarded. This will strengthen the economy year after year, not just shortly after the tax refunds are received.

It is not enough to simply give temporary tax cuts or rebates. Temporary rebates or credits do not lower the price of productive behavior (i.e. work, investment, productivity, entrepreneurship, etcetera). If we want to stimulate the economy, we need to reduce tax rates so that we lower the penalty on productive behavior.

After recent tax cuts, aren't taxes low now?.

The average American family spends more on taxes (federal, state, and local) than on food, clothing, transportation and housing combined. The median two-income family pays nearly 40% of its total income in taxes to federal, state and local government. Yet, the median family spends less than 16% on housing, 4% on clothing, 9% on food and 7% on transportation.

Even after George Bush's 2001 tax cut passed, federal taxes consumed about one-fifth of the entire U.S. economy. During World War II, we financed the free world's defeat of the Axis powers and the reconstruction of Europe and Asia on less. Those who argue that taxes are low and do not need to be reduced are simply divorced from reality.

Do the rich pay their fair share?

One of the oldest and most worn out arguments liberals use against tax cuts is that tax reductions unfairly benefit the rich. Every time a tax cut is proposed, liberals complain that not enough of the benefit goes to the poor. However, when one reduces taxes, one would expect those who pay taxes to benefit. Those who pay more taxes could reasonably be expected to benefit more. Here are the facts. According to the IRS, the top 1% of income earners pay nearly 35% of the total federal income tax burden. The top 10% of earners pay 65% of the taxes. The top 25% of earners pay nearly 83% of the taxes. The bottom 50% of earners pay only 4% of the income taxes. Given these realities, there is no way to cut tax rates and not have it benefit those who pay the taxes.

Perhaps an allegory will explain this point. There was a group of five middle-aged men who were old high school football buddies. They ate lunch together every Wednesday at their favorite restaurant. One of the men was quite wealthy and he began picking up most of the lunch bill—about 80% of the tab. Two of the other fellows, who had good jobs, split the balance of the bill—each paying 10%. Since the bill was now covered, the remaining two friends paid nothing. This was how the other three wanted it, as they knew their two friends were not flush with cash. They kept meeting weekly for several months. One day, the restaurant owner came to the table of these five friends and apologized for overcharging them the past many months and that he owed them a refund of $500. The owner laid five one hundred dollar bills on the table.

The two men who had paid nothing all these months for lunch said, "Hey, this is great, we each get $100." The friends who had actually paid the bill said, "Come on. Be serious. Since we have paid the bills all these months, we should get the refund in proportion to what we paid." The two who had not paid anything became angry and said, "This is not fair. Why should you benefit from the refund and we not share in the benefit? Why are you being so greedy?" Those who had graciously paid the lunch bill for months sat stunned that their friends who had paid nothing thought they should take an equal share of the refund and had the nerve to call them greedy.

And so it is with the federal income tax debate. The left criticizes a tax cut on the basis that those who pay the most will see the greatest reduction. Like the two ungrateful friends, the left seems to think that those who pay little should receive most of the refund. In essence, liberals want tax cuts to be a welfare program.

Do the poor benefit from tax cuts?

Often liberals argue that cutting taxes only helps the rich and that the middle class and the poor are not helped. This is tried and true class warfare—pitting rich against poor and employer against employee. In making this class warfare argument, they ignore the fact that a rising tide lifts all boats. Census Bureau data show that income levels for all income groups—the rich, middle-class and poor—move up and down together. When tax policy rewards work, thrift, investment, entrepreneurship, and income levels go up for everyone—rich and poor alike. When the economy slides into weakness, not surprisingly, all income groups see their income reduced.

The reality is that the poor have the most to gain and lose. When your income barely covers your basic expenses, an increase to your income makes a big difference. And a reduction in your income can be devastating. As a practical matter, the problem with class warfare is that it ignores a rather simple fact—when the rich have more income, they hire, invest and buy more. A poor man has never hired me. Those of us who want a job had better hope that there are a few wealthy folks out there who can afford to hire others and pay them a fair wage.

Do tax cuts cause the deficit to increase?

Every time a tax cut is proposed, the left argues that a tax cut will increase the deficit. However, the deficit is caused because of unrestrained, runaway spending—not because we pay too little taxes. When Reagan cut taxes, Democrats blamed the deficit on him. Yet the federal tax receipts *grew* at an astronomical rate of 28% at least partly as a result of the tax cuts. Unfortunately, spending increased at an even faster pace. Thus, there was a deficit. If spending had increased at a more reasonable rate, there would have been huge surpluses. Yet to liberals, deficits are never caused because they spend too much, but because you and I don't pay enough. Even the current budget deficit is caused primarily because of excessive spending and the economic slowdown that began in 2000.

Very little of the current deficit was caused by Bush's 2001 tax cuts. Yet, if you listen to the left, you would believe that greedy middle class Americans who are paying about 40% of their income to taxes are to blame for the deficit and not Congress who has been spending freely and excessively since the budget was balanced several years ago.

Why does the left reflexively oppose tax cuts?

The bottom line is tax cuts are good for working families, good for the middle-class and even good for the working poor. Liberals oppose tax cuts because those who love big government want more and more money to spend. Tax cuts limit their ability to spend our money on their priorities. They don't care that tax cuts increase our ability to fund our own priorities—education for our children, retirement for our golden years, or a new home. That is because the left is not actually interested in regular folks. They are interested in *their* power, and having more of *our* money to spend—which increases *their* power. Us having more of our own money to spend does nothing for their power, so the left opposes tax cuts out of greedy self-interest.

What adds insult to injury is that they tell us that those who support tax cuts are greedy. Why is it that when we oppose the left's efforts to take more and more of our money, we are called greedy, but when they take our money, they are compassionate and generous?

Whose Mailbox is it Anyway?

(Originally published in June 2003)

Recently, I fixed and painted my old and ailing mailbox. After sanding it, and applying two coats of primer and two coats of black paint, I affixed new numbers representing our street address. It would seem natural that I should maintain and take good care of my mailbox—after all it is mine, right? Wrong. The U.S. Postal Service owns it.

That's right folks. You may have paid for the mailbox. You may have installed it. You may have painted and maintained it. You may own the land on which it sits. It may have your name and address on it, but you do not own it. But you don't control it.

How do I know that you and I don't own our own mailbox? Simple. I was recounting my weekend handyman exploits, including my mailbox painting, to a coworker when she asked if I had saved my receipts to submit to the U.S. Postal Service for reimbursement. I naturally asked why and she explained that my mailbox is actually the Postal Service's mailbox.

She had been handing out a flyer for a school activity to a few of her neighbors. For those who were not home, she placed the flyer in their mailbox. A U.S. Postal Service carrier spotted her and followed her in his postal truck. He then confronted her saying that she could not place anything in a U.S. Postal Service mailbox. My friend naturally pointed out that she was simply placing a school flyer in the mailbox of a few of her friends. The postal carrier's response was instructive, "Listen, lady, your friends don't own these mailboxes. We do."

My coworker and I both knew that one cannot tamper with the mail. We all want the mail to be secure. But placing a school flyer in a mailbox hardly jeopardizes the security or safety of the mail. Moreover, tampering or stealing mail is a separate crime. Quite frankly, there is no sound reason why the Postal Service must claim ownership of my mailbox. All the behavior they want to outlaw (i.e. stealing mail, tampering with mail, sending harmful substances in the mail, etcetera) is already outlawed without them laying claim to my mailbox and trying to control its use. I for one would prefer to have a school flyer or a community notice or even my newspaper placed in my mailbox. They wouldn't get rained on and blown all over the neighborhood and there is plenty of space for these things and my daily mail.

My grandfather always told me, "He who pays the piper, calls the tune." When it comes to my mailbox, I've been paying the piper—I bought the mailbox and installed and maintained it. However, the Postal Service is calling the tune—they control and micromanage the use of my mailbox. I would prefer to use my mailbox to receive my daily newspaper, school flyers and my small packages. But the Postal Service says no—only they can use my mailbox. How many mornings is our newspaper wet? How often does the school flyer get blown around the neighborhood? How many times have we missed the delivery of a package because we are not home? While it makes sense to use my mailbox to better serve my needs, I simply do not have the power under current law to make such choices. There is something wrong with this picture.

The Postal Service, and more to the point, Congress need to recognize that if it is our mailbox (and by any reasonable standard it is), it must be treated as our mailbox. Alternatively, if the Postal Service really wants to own my mailbox, I will consider selling it to them and leasing the small spot of soil on which it sits, and charging them for my maintenance of it.

When Competing Successfully Is a "Crime"

(Originally published in November 1999)

On Friday, November 4th, U.S. District Judge Thomas Penfield Jackson issued a 207-page decision that contained findings of fact in the government's antitrust lawsuit against Microsoft. These findings of fact are not the judge's final ruling on the case—they are simply his findings as to the basic facts in the case. Now attorneys on both sides will spend months arguing how the law applies to the facts and which facts are most important.

Reviewing Judge Jackson's findings of facts makes it clear that he just doesn't get it—and this isn't the first time Judge Jackson failed to get it. Earlier in this same case, an appellate court overturned Jackson and upheld Microsoft's right to design its products as it saw fit. That was not the sort of ruling one would expect a federal judge to get wrong.

Judge Jackson's findings of fact seem premised on the notion that Microsoft is a monopoly. All of this may sound plausible to the uninformed—after all Microsoft is a very large and very successful company. But in reality, most of Judge Jackson's findings of fact are nothing short of absurd. Under the law, being large and successful does not make one a monopoly.

Basic economic theory teaches that monopolies dominate the market and use their monopoly power to, among other things (i) increase prices forcing hapless consumers to dramatically overpay for goods because there is no other option, (ii) slow innovation and development of new technologies and processes so that the monopoly can better maintain its power and profits and (iii) provide inferior products to consumers on the assumption that they have no place else to go. If the federal government and Judge Jackson are correct that Microsoft is a monopoly, it must be the case that Microsoft is (i) increasing prices, (ii) limiting innovation and (iii) providing inferior products. Let's examine the facts and see.

Microsoft products are now cheaper than ever. Every new release of software does more and costs less. Microsoft now gives away its browser and its e-mail and contact management software. They update this free software regularly to improve it and make it more powerful. The updates are also free. How are consumers harmed by less expensive and more powerful software? How are consumers harmed by free software?

The computer industry and the Internet are growing so rapidly and new technologies are being developed at such a dizzying rate that it is virtually impossible that Microsoft has limited innovation. In fact, Microsoft has been a leader in making the Internet more accessible to average-every-day computer users. Moreover, Microsoft has been such a powerful innovator that it has pushed other companies such as Netscape and AOL to improve their products. Who gains when Microsoft's competitors improve their products to keep up with Microsoft? Consumers.

Finally, Microsoft products are among the best in the industry. Monopolies are not typically known for providing the highest quality. Yet, Windows has simplified computer use for millions of people who were intimidated by DOS's cumbersome operating system. Word, Excel, Access, Explorer, Outlook Express and Power Point are industry-leading software applications. The main complaint I've heard about Microsoft products is that they offer too many features and are too powerful. That is like complaining about a dishwasher because it cleans even the dirtiest dishes.

Ask yourself, how are consumers harmed by Microsoft offering improved software for lower prices? How are consumers harmed by Microsoft giving away its web browser? How are consumers harmed by a high-tech environment in which innovation is so rapid that home computers and consumer software now do things that years ago, not even super computers could do? How are consumers harmed by Microsoft pushing companies like AOL and Netscape and other competitors to upgrade and improve their products? How are consumers harmed by being able to purchase high-quality and inexpensive software like Word and Excel?

The answer is painfully simple—there is no harm. In fact, the consumer has been the largest beneficiary of Microsoft's innovation.

It appears that Judge Jackson has spent so much time focusing on arcane and obscure points of law that he missed the basic point—monopolies charge high prices for shoddy goods and prevent others from providing quality goods at reasonable prices. Microsoft has not done any of these things. The record is all too clear. Microsoft has simply worked very hard to produce the best software products available. As a result, we are all winners.

However, some of Microsoft's competitors think that striving for innovation and excellence should be a crime. If those competitors are successful, we all will be the losers. Judge Jackson should keep this in mind before he precedes any further.

AOL—Time Warner Merger Proves that Microsoft is No Threat

(Originally published in January 2000)

The recently announced AOL-Time Warner mega-merger proves that the government never had a serious case against Microsoft. Even if the government's case once had a small kernel of truth, the marketplace and computer and Internet technology are progressing so rapidly that the government's case is now moot.

The AOL-Time Warner merger will break all records with its total estimated value of nearly $350 billion. It will combine AOL, the largest Internet provider in the world and owner of Netscape software, with Time Warner's vast system of broadband Internet technology as well as its media, entertainment and news services. The new AOL-Time Warner company will dwarf most of its competition and will have the resources to take on virtually any project or competitor it chooses. With these facts in mind, how can the government continue to argue that Microsoft exercised monopoly power to bully AOL out of the market?

For the past year and a half, government attorneys warned us in grave tones that Microsoft was and is using its market to hamper its competitors and harm consumers. These charges rang hollow then, but in light of the recently announced mega-merger, the charges have been exposed for the absurdity that they are.

The public should have sensed that it was about to be sucker-punched when the government's attorneys promised to protect us from Microsoft's free and very popular Internet Explorer and Outlook Express. Consumers don't need protection from high quality, free software. However, Americans do need protection from a Justice Department that wastes tax dollars, cheapens the law and abuses government power to benefit some competitors while harming others.

Given the rapid development of technology and swift changes in the marketplace, government attempts to regulate the high-tech computer and Internet market will be ineffectual and irrelevant at best. At worst, such meddling will impede innovation and halt economic growth. In either event, citizens and consumers would be the hardest hit.

The government claims that Microsoft is one of the most powerful and predatory monopolies ever known. Moreover, it now argues that the only solution is to impose the "death penalty" on Microsoft by placing the software company in the government's corporate guillotine—to be broken up into two or three pieces.

Before imposing such a drastic sentence, a brief look at the facts is in order. AOL has the market power and resources to purchase Time Warner in the largest merger ever. The bottom line is rather simple—if Microsoft is the "all powerful" and "evil monopoly" that the government claims, why is AOL able to finance the largest merger ever?

Think back in history—did Standard Oil's competitors have the resources to pull off a $350 billion merger? Of course not. And why? Because Standard Oil had the market power to dominate its competitors and stop such mergers cold. AOL's financial and market strength belies the government's claim that Microsoft exercises monopoly power and squelches competition. At the very least, it is now obvious that the passage of time has made the government's case irrelevant.

This mega-merger provides ample proof that there is, and will continue to be, an abundance of competition in the high-tech computer and Internet arena. Government lawsuits are not needed to promote competition. Such lawsuits only endanger the dynamic and rapidly advancing high-tech economy. Simply stated, it is time for the government to stop its jihad against Microsoft.

One is left to wonder why the government continues to waste its time and the taxpayer's money relentlessly pursuing Microsoft and trying to impose the corporate death penalty. AOL is obviously thriving. Microsoft has not harmed or hampered AOL. In fact, one could now plausibly argue that a large, healthy Microsoft is needed as a counterbalance to the new mega-Internet firm AOL-Time Warner.

If the government lacks the judgment to drop its lawsuit against Microsoft, then Judge Thomas Penfield Jackson should dismiss the government's case as moot and let the competition and innovation continue. Consumers will be the biggest winners.

Law Enforcement by Special Interests: Consumers Lose Again

(Originally published in April 2000)

Judge Thomas Penfield Jackson's Microsoft decision immediately sent the stock market into a record-breaking fall. Fortunately for the market, there was a modest, but spasmodic rebound. While the billions of dollars that were whipped out in one afternoon grabbed most of the headlines, there is one alarming development that has been largely overlooked. The law enforcement responsibilities of both the Department of Justice (DOJ) and the attorneys general from several states have been surrendered to special interests and the highest bidder.

Immediately after the Microsoft settlement talks broke down, it was reported that the terms of the proposed settlement agreement had been shared with Scott McNealy, the chairman of Sun Microsystems, a chief Microsoft rival. Other rivals were also allowed to review and "critique" the terms of the proposed agreement. These rivals were reportedly "alarmed" that the settlement was too limited and did not sufficiently harm Microsoft. These rivals expressed their dissatisfaction to government officials and desire for tougher terms.

Law enforcement is supposed to be above politics and above gamesmanship. It is supposed to be about impartially enforcing and upholding the law. When government becomes involved in antitrust litigation, it is supposed to represent the interests of the American people and consumers—not the direct competitors of the company being investigated.

The government has an awesome enforcement power and is required to enforce the law ethically and impartially. But the Reno Department of Justice and a group of state attorneys general apparently believe they are above the law. Moreover, when the government seeks approval and input about a settlement agreement from the competitors of the company being investigated, it brings into question who the government is actually working for. Are the attorneys general and the Department of Justice trying to satisfy the law or simply appease Microsoft's competitors? Unfortunately, the facts speak for themselves.

Let's get one point straight from the start—it would be normal and completely ethical if government officials had merely interviewed witnesses in competing companies to determine the facts of this case. However, government officials were not learning the facts when they colluded with the competitors of Microsoft. This litigation has been in progress for several years. The fact-finding phase of the trial ended a long time ago. Months ago, Judge Jackson issued an exhaustive, phonebook-sized document called the "findings of fact." At this point, the parties know the facts.

The collusion between government officials and competitors of Microsoft was about one thing—did Microsoft's competitors find the proposed settlement satisfactory? Or more bluntly stated, did the settlement agreement sufficiently damage Microsoft so that its competitors were confident that they could seize upon some business advantage?

It is nothing short of outrageous that competitors would be asked if they thought that the settlement agreement was "rough enough" on Microsoft. If you were a competitor of Microsoft—no penalty, no matter how severe, and no fine, no matter how high, would be satisfactory. If they had their way, the government would put Microsoft out of business, sell its assets at a public auction and then give the proceeds to Microsoft's competitors.

What makes this entire unsavory lapse of law and ethics even worse is that Microsoft's competitors can use the legal findings from the government's case in their own follow-up lawsuits against Microsoft. Thus, the government has in a very real way become the co-counsel with Microsoft's competitors. Again, who is the Justice Department representing? Who are the attorneys general representing? Whose interests are they pursuing? Consumers? Or competitors?

Antitrust enforcement is not about satisfying or appeasing the competitors of a company being investigated. It is about protecting consumers from monopolies. But, consumers do not need protection from Microsoft. Computers and software are now cheaper, more powerful and more user-friendly than ever—in large part due to Microsoft's innovations. Microsoft gives away its web browser and e-mail program for free. Microsoft's other products such as Word, Excel and Power Point are extremely popular because they are powerful, easy to use, and relatively inexpensive. As a consumer, I do not want protection from high quality software that is either free or inexpensive.

The recent actions of government officials in the Microsoft case go well beyond the law and any standard of acceptable ethics. Unfortunately, consumers are the biggest losers.

"Too much" Innovation Now Dubbed Predatory Innovation

(Originally published in May 2000)

Over the past two weeks, we have witnessed the Clinton-Gore Justice Department, Microsoft competitors and Judge Thomas Penfield Jackson arguing over whether chopping Microsoft into two or three pieces would be the "best outcome." "Best" for whom? Government lawyers trying to make a name for themselves? Microsoft competitors trying to gain some advantage through harassing litigation?

Historically, antitrust law has been used to stop monopolists from fixing prices, foisting shoddy goods on customers, colluding with other businesses and other similar anti-competitive misdeeds. The law has never been used to punish a successful company for aggressively improving its products. Yet, the fear that Microsoft has improved its products too much and innovated too rapidly is at the heart of the Justice Department's case and Judge Jackson's findings of fact.

The Justice Department and Judge Jackson complain that Microsoft invests about 17% of its gross profits in research and development (R&D). They say that compared to other companies, this percentage is high. Then they conclude that Microsoft has engaged in "predatory" innovation. Simply stated, the Justice Department and Judge Jackson believe that Microsoft sought to sell more software by making it better. Oddly, they think this is bad—labeling it "predatory innovation."

The Justice Department and Judge Jackson are correct that Microsoft reinvests a lot of its profits in R&D. But why they think this is bad is a mystery. When a company reinvests its profits in R&D, consumers get better products. Simply stated, Microsoft's strong investment in R&D is good news, not grounds for predatory litigation by the Justice Department.

Judge Jackson and the Justice Department fear that all this innovation and improvement may have harmed Microsoft's competitors—presumably because these competitors were not improving their software or innovating as rapidly. The whole concept behind competitive markets is that companies compete with each other to bring to market the best products at the best price. Consumers benefit when competing companies are trying to "out-do" each other.

It is a good thing Judge Jackson and the Clinton-Gore Justice Department were not around when Henry Ford was innovating with automobiles and assembly lines. They would have said it was predatory innovation to give consumers new "horseless carriages" at such low prices. How could Henry Ford's competitors keep up with such innovations? Even worse, buggy and carriage companies suffered losses and finally went out of business. According to the Justice Department and Judge Jackson, this sort of innovation is harmful. Again I ask, to whom? Consumers benefited greatly.

Or how about Thomas Edison? We are fortunate that Judge Jackson and the Clinton-Gore Justice Department were not around to stop one of the most predatory innovations of the modern age—the light bulb. Companies that provided light by oil, gas and candles simply could not keep up with Edison's innovation. Extending the thinking of the Justice Department and Judge Jackson demonstrates how utterly silly it is.

Innovations—whether the light bulb, the automobile, the airplane, the computer or computer software—benefit consumers. Innovation is not something to bemoan. It should be celebrated. But not at the Clinton-Gore Justice Department, not in Judge Jackson's court and certainly not by Microsoft's competitors.

Unfortunately, consumers will pay a heavy price for the Justice Department's predatory antitrust enforcement. So far, all the Clinton-Gore team has done with their jihad against innovation is drive the stock market sharply down. The market understands what is happening—even if Clinton, Gore, Reno and Judge Jackson don't. The market is expressing its concern that government lawyers and regulators have run amok and decided that punishing innovation is a good idea. The market is demonstrating its rational apprehension that once these folks finish with Microsoft, they will move on to feed on other companies guilty of "too much" innovation—whatever that means. Henry Ford and Thomas Edison should be glad they never met the Clinton-Gore Justice Department or Judge Jackson. If they had, we'd still be reading by candlelight and riding in horse drawn carriages. After all, too much innovation can be a dangerous thing.

The States are the Bullies

(Originally published in June 2002)

The United States Department of Justice settled its lawsuit with Microsoft last year. Most of the states involved in the litigation joined in the settlement. Yet, eight states (California, Connecticut, Florida, Iowa, Kansas, Massachusetts, Minnesota and Utah) and Washington D.C. refused to accept the settlement and decided to continue the litigation. They have now made their closing arguments—arguing primarily that Microsoft is a corporate bully and that the states have no choice but to continue this litigation into its sixth year. The states' shrill warnings of bullying are not convincing. It is the states and their attorneys who are the bullies.

First, the states don't have a good a case. The federal government litigated these issues for five years and last year received an adverse ruling from a federal appeals court. So, the federal government settled the case with Microsoft and most of the states involved. However, eight states and D.C. decided that the settlement was not good enough and that the litigation needed to continue. They wanted more cash to cover their budget shortfalls and they needed to protect their citizens from free web browsers.

Second, the states are the bullies in this case, not Microsoft. The states have powerful attorneys general and hundreds of staff attorneys. Using tax dollars, they have an almost unlimited ability to litigate. The rest of the world—including Microsoft—must pay for their own lawyers and have a strong incentive to settle disputes in hopes of saving money. But if the states run up big legal bills, they can simply require you and me to pay more taxes. The rest of us don't have that advantage.

However, I have personal experience with the states' bullying character. On Christmas Eve, the states' attorneys sent me a thirty page subpoena demanding that Frontiers of Freedom—the non-profit public policy foundation that employees me—turn over all its financial records, organizational and corporate records, letters and correspondence, phone records and other files and papers from the last several years. The states' attorneys claimed they wanted to inspect our private records and papers because they ludicrously claimed to believe we were "a repository of evidence" in their antitrust lawsuit against Microsoft.

However, no reasonably intelligent person could have honestly believed our non-profit public policy foundation was a "repository of evidence" in this massive antitrust case. We comment on, write about and critique matters of public policy. We deal with a number of issues—including national security, the environment, property rights, economic policy, constitutional rights and civil justice reform. We have criticized the litigation against Microsoft, questioned the motives of those pushing the litigation and discussed the litigation's impact on the economy. Regardless of whether you agree with our position, no one can dispute that we have a constitutional right to speak on matters of public policy.

We were puzzled why the states responsible for continuing the Microsoft litigation into its sixth year would, at the last minute, subpoena our public policy foundation and demand that we produce a wide variety of private documents and records. What possible evidence could we provide in this lawsuit? None.

The truth is the subpoena was designed to punish us for questioning their legal tactics and to silence us, rather than to obtain evidence. We are not a party to the litigation. We have no contractual relationships with any of the parties in this litigation. We have no evidence relevant to the issues being litigated. We are simply a non-profit foundation that comments on public policy issues. And the states' attorneys did not like our comments. This was their way of punishing us for effectively communicating the weakness of their case and the crassness of their motives.

Our opinions about the states' questionable legal position and tactics, while well-founded, are not evidence in this litigation. Were it otherwise, O.J. Simpson could have subpoenaed average Americans—as retribution for believing he was guilty—demanding that they give him stacks of private information and financial records claiming that those who hold unfavorable opinions of him are a "repository of evidence." However, what you and I think or say about O.J. is not evidence in his murder trial.

While it was flattering that our articles and remarks criticizing the states' legal position generated so much interest from the Attorneys General from California, Connecticut, Florida, Iowa, Kansas, Massachusetts, Minnesota, Utah and Washington D.C., it is clear that they were engaged in an underhanded power play, an unethical abuse of the courts and were trying to bully us—all in an attempt to silence us. So when the states' complain of bullying, forgive me if I laugh. The states are the bullies in this process.

It's the Economy, Energy and the Environment, Stupid

(Originally published in August 2001)

Almost a decade ago, Bill Clinton and Al Gore won the White House repeating the mantra "It's the economy, stupid." Unfortunately, they spent the next eight years making sure that what fuels our economy—energy—was scarce, expensive and derived more and more from unreliable foreign sources. The results are plain and indisputable—during the last eighteen months of the Clinton-Gore Administration the economy was slowing and our energy woes were mounting. In the end, Clinton and Gore hampered the very economy that they were so quick to take credit for.

While taking credit for good times, Clinton and Gore made it virtually impossible to drill for oil in the United States, so now we are dependent on foreign oil for virtually two-thirds of our supply. They added substantially to the regulatory regime that has made it virtually impossible to build new power plants. As a result, states like California where population has been growing are now suffering shortages and astronomical price hikes. Clinton and Gore also spearheaded the Kyoto-Protocol—a UN sponsored treaty based on junk science and apocalyptic predictions—which would mandate an almost 40% reduction in energy use.

Simply put, the Clinton-Gore administration relentlessly pursued an anti-energy policy that is costing us today—not merely in terms of rolling blackouts, brownouts, skyrocketing electric and heating bills and high gasoline prices. The cost is also reflected in the slowing economy, lost jobs, reduced consumer confidence and falling financial markets.

This problem was more than eight years in the making. And it won't be solved overnight. But we can turn things around. There are at least five things that President Bush and Vice President Cheney must do to get our energy, environmental and economic policy back on track.

First, pursue a comprehensive energy policy that includes a wide variety of sources—coal, gas, oil, hydro-, nuclear, renewables, biomass, etcetera. The United States must increase its capacity to produce oil, gas and coal and increase our capacity for the generation of electricity. We cannot continue to rely upon inherently unreliable foreign sources for our energy needs. To those who argue that we cannot develop our own oil for fear of harming the environment, we must be willing to share the facts. For example, in the case of the proposed drilling in the Arctic National Wildlife Refuge (ANWR), the total footprint for drilling would be less than 2000 acres out of almost 20 million acres—the equivalent of a postage stamp on a football field. The United States can develop its energy resources *and* protect the environment.

Second, recognize that while conservation should be a part of any energy policy, the emphasis should be on increasing our energy capacity and infrastructure. The last twenty years have been spent focusing on conservation. It is time to focus on energy availability and affordability. We cannot conserve ourselves into a strong economy or national security.

Third, defeat the Kyoto Protocol and any effort to regulate carbon dioxide (CO_2). The Kyoto Protocol (a.k.a. the UN Global Warming Treaty) and the suggestion that we regulate carbon dioxide are based on junk science and would make any rational energy policy completely impossible. If we regulate carbon dioxide, we don't need an energy policy. The regulation of carbon dioxide would be our energy policy—a policy aimed at limiting and reducing the use and availability of energy and dramatically increasing its cost.

Fourth, integrate energy and environmental policy and make them compatible instead of at cross-purposes. Environmental policy almost always trumps and negates energy policy. We must create a unified policy that promotes affordable energy while being environmentally responsible.

Fifth, stand tough. The White House must not allow the left to deter it with well-orchestrated attacks that it is not environmentally friendly. There is no pleasing the extreme environmental left. They will be critical of any reasonable energy or environmental policy. The left does not care that new technologies permit environmentally responsible energy and resource development. These are the same folks who endorse and promote shoplifting from stores that sell products they don't like such as wood. The bottom line is do not waste time trying to please extremists. It can't be done and even if it could, you wouldn't want to live with the results.

President George W. Bush has his work cut of for him. But, as a nation, we must move with purpose and speed to promote a sound and balanced energy policy that will support our economy, provide for our growing energy needs and protect the environment. After all, it's not just the economy—it's the economy, energy and the environment, stupid.

Pharmaceuticals: Facts Make Things Look Different

(Originally published in October 2001)

Something strange is going on in Washington, D.C. where rhetorical babble ruled the roost through the first eight months of this year.

The anthrax attack that killed two postal workers, left two others in critical condition and closed down Capitol Hill has accentuated just how vital an innovative and prosperous pharmaceutical industry is to America's national security.

Before the September 11th attacks, a number of demagogic politicians regularly taunted the nation's pharmaceutical manufacturers—criticizing them for costs among other things.

Now these taunts have been replaced by pleas to speed up production of existing vaccines and develop new vaccines and medicines to meet potential chemical and biological threats. Familiar companies like Bayer, Pfizer, Eli Lilly, Merck, Upjohn, Pharmacia, and Johnson & Johnson are no longer easy targets.

In truth, pharmaceutical companies were among the first to step up as the World Trade Center towers came crashing down. Since that horrific moment, the industry—a good portion of it concentrated in northern New Jersey—has contributed more than $100 million in cash to relief efforts and many millions more in goods and services.

Bayer, of course, makes Cipro, the antibiotic pills given to the lawmakers and congressional staff members exposed to deadly anthrax spores. Other pharmaceutical manufacturers have stepped up production of anthrax and smallpox vaccines. Still others are working to find vaccines and drugs that thwart the variations of biological and chemical warfare for which there are yet no remedies.

Few of today's miracle drugs would have been developed if U.S. pharmaceutical firms had been laboring under the cruel regulatory restrictions European governments impose on their pharmaceutical companies.

As a result, innovative research & development has withered in nations like Great Britain, France, Switzerland and Germany that once were industry leaders. Today only four European prescription drugs are ranked among the top twenty-five best sellers, with U.S. companies accounting for almost all of the others.

Politicians who dumped on the pharmaceutical industry for increasing prices studiously failed to note that, in many cases, the new drugs significantly lower overall hospital costs by eliminating major surgeries and lengthy hospital stays.

In the future, teaming with biotech companies like Monsanto and Amgen, the pharmaceutical industry likely will be able to deliver important nutrients, medicines and vaccines to the estimated two billion people around the globe now afflicted with lethal diseases or suffering from chronic malnutrition.

Consider this: Even if an effective AIDS vaccine were available today, it would be impossible to deliver en masse to the tens of millions who've contracted the disease in Africa and Asia because there is no public health and transportation infrastructure in place.

Then imagine the wonders that could be worked to alleviate human suffering if such medicines could be delivered through food staples such as corn or cassava or rice.

In the case of Golden Rice, a genetically engineered grain loaded with Vitamin A, it's already being done. As the new rice becomes more prevalent in diets across Asia, cases of Vitamin A deficiency, which currently kills an estimated two million children a year and blinds some 500,000 annually, will plummet.

Drug industry bashing has been a staple of the healthcare debate on Capitol Hill in recent years.

Proponents of greater federal involvement—with war cries of "price gougers" and "unconscionable profiteers"—championed legislation to provide prescription drug coverage for all of the nation's 36 million seniors under a vastly expanded Medicare program—including the more than two-thirds with satisfactory private plans.

Other lawmakers pushed proposals to allow Americans to reimport lower-priced prescription drugs from Canada, Mexico and other countries—despite warnings from health officials of counterfeiting and potential tampering. Now, almost everyone realizes that such legislation also would open the door for terrorists to create even more disasters.

America's pharmaceutical industry has extended extraordinary help in the current crisis and it has provided longstanding leadership in helping the world's six billion-plus people enjoy better health. I realize that like any business in a free-market economy, pharmaceutical companies don't do good solely for the sake of doing good. They produce better products because they're competing in a global marketplace. They want to produce better products at better prices than their competitors. As a result, we all benefit. That is how free markets work. It benefits us all. In a capitalistic system such as ours, those are the only major incentives they really need.

Obviously, there should be wise and intelligent regulation of prescription drugs, but there is a danger in overdoing it. What we don't need from government is a minefield of regulatory disincentives. We want pharmaceutical companies to have ample incentive to create tomorrow's cures and medicines. Thus, bureaucrats should *not* be dictating prices here or abroad or picking winners and losers among the industry. And no one in Congress should be seeking to tax pharmaceutical research and development into oblivion.

Hopefully the demagogic attacks on corporate America by ultra-left politicians will die out like an eradicated disease—simply because the vast majority of Americans have become immune to such hyperbole.

Enron, Monopolies and Corporate Welfare

(Originally published in February 2002)

The term "corporate welfare" is often taken to mean the giving of tax dollars to corporate interests, and sometimes that does happen. But far more frequent, dangerous and insidious is when the government sets up rules and regulations that favor particular corporations over others. Just slant the rules, cook the books, and insert this or that favor-granting clause in the law or regulation or treaty.

That's what Enron was lobbying for in Congress and the Clinton administration. It tried to do the same with the Bush administration, but simply could not get the favors it needed. Enron was a big supporter of the Kyoto Global Warming Treaty. Enron built its business plan on the Treaty's energy rationing regulatory scheme. Then Enron pushed government hard to put rules and regulations into place that would benefit Enron. Bush refused to give Enron the "corporate welfare" it sought.

Although sad for their unknowing investors, Enron probably got what it deserved—bankruptcy—when it proved that without special government favors, it could not compete in the free market. The Kyoto Global Warming Treaty was not ratified—the government wouldn't give Enron what it was hoping for. As a result, Enron went belly up because it had banked on profiting handsomely from the new regulatory scheme mandated by the Kyoto Treaty.

Other corporations, too, sometimes try to enhance their market position by seeking special government favors, and it is the special obligation of conservatives to oppose those efforts whenever and wherever they occur.

Right now, one of the most significant special-favor lobbying efforts is being mounted by the government-created regional telephone monopolies. These monopolies owe their very existence to the Federal government, and are at present trying to get their favored status enhanced and extended through legislation known in Washington as the Tauzin-Dingell bill.

These companies were once known as the "Baby Bells," but they've grown into such unruly monopolists, that they can no longer be considered "babies." And, just like Enron, they're trying to use their power and influence in Washington to corrupt the free market and fix the rules in their favor.

Here's what's going on. Way back in 1984, before the advent of sophisticated cell phone networks, the Internet or even the widespread use of personal computers, a Federal Judge created regional monopoly companies to offer local telephone service with profits guaranteed through state public utility commissions. These regional phone monopolies were prohibited from offering long distance service. Long distance therefore became a true free market, and in classic form quickly developed robust competition between AT&T, MCI, Sprint and dozens of other smaller but often successful companies. And just as conservatives predicted, consumer prices dropped dramatically. Such is the power of the free market.

In 1996, the Telecommunications Act—a bill designed to bring the benefits of the free market to local telephone service—was signed into law. Under this law, the regional phone monopolies were required to sell to new competing phone companies access to phone system infrastructure at reasonable prices. Since the phone lines were built with government-guaranteed profits, the plan was to require the monopolists to allow access to the phone line infrastructure. This was designed to build competition for local phone services. In return for this concession from the monopolists, the law lifted the restriction that prohibited the regional phone monopolists from going into the long distance business and a variety of Internet services.

The Bell companies wanted the benefit of entering the long distance and Internet services marketplace. It promised to be widely profitable. But they also wanted to retain their monopoly. In other words, the Bells wanted the benefits, but did not want to pay the costs. Thus, the Bells reacted to the new law in two ways.

First, they did everything in their power to delay and frustrate the new competitive local phone service companies that sprang up in the wake of the law's passage. A customer would sign up with new phone Company X, which would then go to the Bell monopoly and pay to access its network as guaranteed by law. Months later, Company X's phone service still wouldn't be working right because of the Bell company's lack of cooperation. The customer would be mad at Company X and in many cases the customer would switch back to the Bell monopoly. The sabotage worked well. Lots of new Company X competitors went bankrupt in the process.

Second, the Bells stepped up their efforts to get portions of the 1996 law repealed. They got friendly congressmen to give them the ability to expand and maintain their monopoly, backed it with an amazing lobbying effort that cost millions of dollars, and spent big bucks on political contributions. Two of the Bells were among the top eight corporate Political Action Committees (PACs) in total contributions to candidates in recent elections.

Enron has nothing on the regional phone companies when it comes to seeking government favors and "corporate welfare." Tauzin-Dingell is a massive corporate welfare giveaway to the Bully Bells, which have used their financial, legal and political power to stall implementation of the market-opening provisions of the 1996 law for six years. Now they want to cash in their political chips and have Congress kill those market opening requirements—and any competition for local service—altogether.

The bill would accelerate the re-monopolization of the U.S. telecom market, which would mean higher prices and fewer choices, exactly the opposite of what Congress promised when the Telecom Act was passed in 1996.

No one should be fooled by the Bell's rhetoric that all they want is a free market. That's not what they want. What they want is the perpetuation of their government-created monopolies with government-guaranteed profits and new government rules that will keep out competition.

Congress can strike a victory for consumers and the free market by deep-sixing legislation that provides special favors to powerful monopolies.

States Go Taxing for Dollars

(Originally published in March 2002)

After more than a year of a lagging economy, a number of states are strapped for tax dollars. For most of us, less income means we spend less. But for government that is rarely the case. Rather than tighten their belts like the rest of us, government tends to look for creative ways to take more of our money. For example, some states have decided that continuing the years of litigation against Microsoft is a good way to generate revenues. Another approach some states are considering is increasing tobacco taxes, again.

Let me state up front that I don't own Microsoft or tobacco stock and I don't smoke. But as an American, I think it would be a good idea if state governments live by the same rules the rest of us live by. Government needs to learn to get by on less. Everyone else is reducing expenditures. But not government. Politicians prefer the rest of us to dig deeper into our pockets so that they don't have to control their spending.

With respect to the several states that persist in suing Microsoft, we are told that the litigation is to protect consumers. This is simply an attempt to make a lousy lawsuit sound laudable. Regardless of what one thinks of Microsoft's marketing, one is hard-pressed to argue that giving away free e-mail applications and web browsers harms consumers. It is rather clear that the states that continue to pursue Microsoft are only protecting the state's ability to spend other people's money.

Yet despite this rather obvious point, we are told that spending our tax dollars on continued litigation is for our benefit. Oh really? First, we pay for the government's attorneys to litigate a pointless case. Second, we will have to pay for this screwy litigation again either because software costs more so that the developers can afford to pay their attorneys or we pay because of the harm this litigation has inflicted on the economy, jobs, retirement accounts and the stock market. People are freaking out about the economic harm caused by Enron's collapse, yet the economic harm caused by the government's relentless pursuit of Microsoft has been at least 10 times greater. Enough is enough.

With respect to tobacco, folks who support raising tobacco taxes generally say, "Tobacco needs to pay its fair share of taxes." Who could disagree with that? Everyone should pay their fair share of taxes. However, what is a fair share? The average farmer can earn about $1,400 from an acre of tobacco. So if the government gets half that much, would that be fair? After all, the government isn't doing any of the work. Or how about if the government got $1,400 from that acre of tobacco? Would that be fair?

Here are the facts. While the average farmer can earn $1,400 from an acre of tobacco, the government (local, state and federal) collects over $60,000 from that same acre of tobacco. So, to all those who want tobacco to pay its "fair share," I ask, is more than $60,000 per acre enough to satisfy your demands for fairness? If not, what amount would satisfy you?

The government collects about 43 times what a farmer makes off the same acre of tobacco. But, how about "Big Tobacco" you ask? In 2000, a tobacco company made about 28 cents per pack of cigarettes sold in New York City. The government (federal, state and local) collected over $1.20 per pack. So government makes 400% what "Big Tobacco" makes and the government does nothing but collect the taxes. So who is greedy? "Big Tobacco" or "Big Government?"

New York City Mayor Michael Bloomberg recently released his budget plan and it included increasing the city tax on cigarettes from 8 cents per pack to $1.50 per pack. This new increase along with increases in the state cigarette tax would push cigarette prices to about $7 per pack in New York City.

This is simply government run amok. If they can tax a pack of cigarettes into the $7 per pack price range, they can tax anything else as well. There are those who argue government should tax foods based on their fat content. I simply do not want the government involved in helping me choose what I eat for dinner. I don't want them rewarding me for eating my vegetables and I don't want them punishing me for eating cheesecake. Those are decisions that the government should not be involved in.

It is time for government to STOP looking at companies and industries with deep pockets as if they were a resource to be strip-mined. When times get tough, the rest of us have to make adjustments. We cannot rob our neighbors or break-in to a local business to cover our shortfalls through thievery. There is no reason why government should do this either.

Trade Authority Benefits Workers and the Economy

(Originally published in January 2003)

Ever since Marco Polo traveled from Venice to China more than seven centuries ago, bringing back silk, porcelain and other exotic goods to his fellow Europeans, mankind has instinctively known the value of trade. In more modern times, innumerable academic studies—not to speak of practical observation—have shown that more trade means more jobs, more available goods and greater overall economic activity. Given our wealth of knowledge about the benefits of trade, you would think that the American government would be doing everything possible to advance trade today.

Unfortunately, that is not the case.

American efforts to promote trade are hamstrung by the fact that the President of the United States—unlike many of his counterparts around the globe—does not have authority to negotiate trade agreements with other countries. President Bush wants to change that because he knows that American workers would be the winners. The proposal he's now advancing is that the president be given authority to negotiate trade deals, which would then be subject to acceptance by Congress on a straight "up or down" vote.

It's not such a radical idea. In fact, every president since Gerald Ford has had this authority, but it lapsed in 1994 and has not been reinstated. President Bush is just one of millions of Americans who say it's time to rectify that. Why? The president said it best when he recently declared that, "History has shown that expanded trade—imports as well as exports—leads to more prosperous U.S. businesses, more choices of goods and lower prices for consumers, and more opportunities for American farmers and workers leading to higher wages, more jobs and economic growth."

Granting trade promotion authority to the president will spur that economic growth by opening markets for U.S. exporters through a new round of global trade negotiations in the World Trade Organization, the Free Trade Area of the Americas and in bilateral trade agreements. Millions of Americans would like to see that happen. They support this move for a very simple reason—they know that trade is essential to the American economy because they work in jobs created by that trade. In fact, twelve million Americans work at jobs that depend on exports of goods and services. And those exports constitute a huge part of the American economy. Last year alone, the United States exported $780 billion in goods and services to more than 200 markets around the world. The agricultural sector alone exported $51 billion in products and crops last year, supporting 750,000 jobs in the process.

These figures are impressive and might lead one to conclude that America is doing fine on the world stage of trade. The risk of such a conclusion is that this complacency could leave America standing still just as other nations are stepping up their efforts to expand trade. In such an environment, the lack of trade promotion authority for the president places American exporters at a disadvantage. How so?

When industrial and consumer products become tariff-free to consumers in other countries, they buy more of our products. When tariffs artificially drive our prices up, foreign consumers buy less. It is simply a matter of pricing. If a donut costs 40¢, I buy several or maybe even a dozen. If a donut costs $3 due to taxes and tariffs, I look elsewhere. Obviously, donuts are not a big export product in the American economy, but heavy machinery and equipment, automobiles and automobile parts, tools, computer products, software, medical equipment, wood and paper products, and agricultural products are big export items.

Here's an example of how free trade helps American workers and America's economy. Let's suppose Chile wants to buy billions of dollars of heavy equipment, computers, and medical equipment. Brazil, Canada and the United States are the primary competitors for Chile's business. In this example, there is a 2% tariff on goods exported from Brazil to Chile. Canada has a free trade agreement with Chile so there is no tariff added to the price of their goods. Without a free trade agreement, American goods would be slapped with an 8% tariff. Under this system, Chilean buyers find goods from Canada and Brazil are much less expensive than goods from America.

Who gets Chile's business? Canada and Brazil. American firms lose sales and profits and are forced to downsize. Employees are laid off. Some firms eventually move part their American operations to foreign countries to avoid the unfavorable trade tariffs and thus sell more of their goods abroad.

None of this is good for America or American workers. High tariffs only reduce our exports of quality American-made goods and increase our export of quality American jobs. Free trade is the antidote for this problem.

Granting trade promotion authority to the president would not only help eliminate the prospect of lost export-related jobs, it would create more jobs in the process by expanding trade. The farmers, ranchers and workers of America deserve the full support and effort of their government in that mission. That is why Congress should move promptly to reinstate this authority to the office of the presidency. The clock is ticking and American workers should not be forced to wait any longer.

How to Preserve America's Status as the Breadbasket of the World

(Originally published in May 2004)

More than thirty years ago, when I was in elementary school, I was taught that America was the breadbasket of the world. I've finished school, but last night I was helping my daughter study for a test on farm life in the 19th Century. As much as my life has changed, agriculture has changed even more. But if we are not careful, America will cease to be the world's breadbasket.

The agricultural economy is suffering due to burdensome regulations and a social climate that is biased against modern agricultural operations and biotechnology. The United States is on the verge of becoming a net-importer of agricultural products. If we are not careful, we will import our food at the same levels we import our oil. Given our fertile farmland, that would be like Saudi Arabia importing oil. Here are five principles that will strengthen America's agricultural economy.

1. Reasonable and consistent environmental regulation.

Government has an important role to play in ensuring that the environment is protected. Farmers have an equal stake in maintaining a healthy environment. However, too often government solutions have imposed specific command and control solutions, rather than setting standards for a clean and safe environment. This command and control approach has cost billions of dollars, slowed economic and environmental innovation, weakened the economy, killed jobs, enriched trail lawyers and, as often as not, failed to protect the environment.

There is a popular misconception that the private sector is in natural opposition to the environment. Yet, if that is true, why is it that endangered species are most often found on private land? The answer is simple—privately held lands generally provide a better habitat—which means that private landholders are generally more environmentally friendly.

When the government sets reasonable and scientifically supportable standards for air quality, water purity and other environmental matters, they protect the environment, but allow the private sector to try different approaches and technologies to achieve the goal of a clean and safe environment. This has the advantage of ensuring a clean environment, while maximizing innovation and strengthening the economy. Environmental protection must be based on reasonable cost-benefit analysis and sound science, and be carried out equitably and enforced through a partnership with farms and business.

2. Reasonable and consistent operational regulations.

Regulations are generally intended to serve some worthwhile purpose or goal. But when regulations are unreasonable, they can choke efficiency and make production unprofitable. In the former Soviet Union, most of the agriculture products of the country were produced on small private plots while the vast government regulated farms failed to produce enough food to feed the populace. If regulation were a necessary element to productive farms, the Soviet-run farms would have been among the most productive. Yet, Soviet farms were remarkable only for their lack of productivity.

This is not to say that all regulation is bad. For example, carefully placed and timed traffic lights can improve safety and the flow of traffic. But putting a traffic light at every street corner would be costly and counterproductive—slowing the flow of traffic rather than aiding it. The same is true of regulating agriculture. While some regulations may be needed, more is not necessarily better. Regulations should be based on the best available science, tailored to be the least restrictive way to accomplish the needed goal and be implemented for a period of time that allows the regulations to be tested and evaluated so that productive regulations can be continued and regulations that failed to achieve their stated purposes or proved to be more costly than estimated can be sunsetted or revised.

3. Promote policies that embrace global free trade.

The marketplace is global. The agriculture sector must be able to sell its products overseas. When we encourage innovation, free trade works. When we create burdensome rules and dictate a one-size-fits-all approach, American producers struggle to compete and do poorly in the global marketplace. Vigorous trade is vital to the health of our economy. Twelve million Americans work at jobs that depend on exports. The agriculture sector alone exported $51 billion in products last year, supporting 750,000 jobs in the process.

Here is a concrete example of how free trade can help American producers. Canada has preferential trade agreements with Chile. An $187,000 Caterpillar 140 H Motor Grader tractor made in America is slapped with tariffs of 8% when it enters Chile. This adds a whopping $14,960 to the cost of the tractor. The same tractor made in Canada faces zero tariffs when shipped to Chile.

The net result of this is that rather than exporting tractors to Chile, we export jobs to Canada. Exporting tractors is good business. Exporting high paying skilled jobs is not. The United States can and will continue its dominance in agriculture by pushing for free trade and policies that encourage domestic production.

4. The government should not dictate business plans and approaches.

Imagine what would have happen if the home computer industry were strictly regulated as to means of production. Government would have determined how computers were to be built and what features they were to have. The regulations would likely reflect technology at the time the regulations were put into place. But this would create an almost insurmountable blockade to further innovation. Thus, had government regulated computer production, we would all be using computers that were slow, had yellow or green monitors, had limited storage capacity and slow modem connections. We would not have computers that play digital quality music, store and organize digital photos, play movies, surf the net or could be put in our brief case and taken places.

But because the government did not meddle in the marketplace, innovation thrived. Small and large companies pursuing different strategies developed cutting edge technologies that lead to major break-throughs. Some companies focused on software. Others on hardware. Still others on the integration of hardware and software. As a result, middle class Americans now have home computers that in 1965 not even the federal government could afford.

The same is true in agriculture. Agricultural producers have varied business plans and should be afforded the flexibility to execute those plans. Too often government places burdensome regulations on certain types of production because of the size of their operations. For example, there is proposed legislation to prevent meat packers from owning livestock or to treat them differently through regulation. Government should not limit the options of producers, nor legislate a bias for or against certain production methods—big or small, independent or contract. Proposals attempting to regulate the marketplace by banning these relationships are not wise or sustainable and are a step toward protectionism instead of free markets.

5. Improve the "political and social" climate for agriculture.

When asked where food comes from, far too many Americans respond "the grocery store." For most Americans, what they think about the farm is more based on some old black and white television rerun than reality. Many Americans mistakenly think of agriculture as a low-tech endeavor involving dirt, water, fertilizer, livestock and tractors. But the reality is that agriculture is a high-tech field, using global positioning systems, computers, weather satellites, complex chemistry, microbiology and genetics.

Many Americans do not realize that today they spend a great deal less of their income feeding their family than their grandparents did. Why? Because of the efficiency and productivity of free markets. Today's farmers produce more at a much lower cost.

America will maintain its strong global agricultural position as long as we have pro-agriculture policies that encourage innovation, reward efficiency, allow the most efficient means of production and allow farmers, ranchers and others in the agriculture sector to sell their products to the world.

4

National Security and Foreign Policy

Peace through Strength

(Originally published in May 2004)

George Washington, the only U.S. president to be elected by a unanimous vote—not once, but twice—wisely said, "To be prepared for war is one of the most effectual means of preserving peace." George Washington understood that peace is achieved through strength and conversely, that weakness invites attack.

Today George Washington's counsel is wiser than ever before. Even a casual review of current events makes it clear that the risk of a missile attack is greater than ever. North Korea and China have and continue to develop missiles that can strike the United States. North Korea has threatened on more than one occasion to use its weapons—with those threats being aimed primarily at the United States. China has made not so subtle threats as well. Iran has missiles that can reach American military bases and is seeking more technology to expand its reach. Additionally, terrorists are scouring the black markets to purchase such missiles and missile technology.

On September 11, 2001, al Qaeda did not have real missiles so they used airliners filled with jet fuel as their missiles. It takes little imagination to determine what terrorists intend to do with the weapons they seek. A single missile packs a much greater punch than a mere airliner loaded with jet fuel. As horrific as September 11th was, if missiles had been used instead of airliners, it would have been much worse—unimaginably worse.

The risks are real and they are increasing every day. These are not wild-eyed pessimistic fears—they are legitimate risk assessments. Given these risks, what should we do? George Washington's advice provides the only sensible solution—get prepared and be strong and resolute. We have the ability to build and deploy a robust layered missile defense system. Technologically, we can do it. Those who argue that building a missile defense system is not feasible simply do not understand our capability.

It is not a question of technological ability, but rather of political will. We have the technological ability, but we have lacked the political will to do what is necessary. We could have had a missile defense system in place now, had the 1990s not been squandered. During most of the previous decade, the White House and many in Congress argued that missile defense was not needed and thus, it was not seriously funded or pursued. As a result, to this day we cannot protect Americans from missile attack.

Fortunately, President George W. Bush and many in Congress today understand that having an effective defense against missile attack has never been more important. The President has said that by late 2004, we will have the first elements of a missile defense in place and functional. But there are still too many in the halls of Congress who would rather pursue their pet pork projects than adequately fund missile defense.

Thus, one of the most important issues facing America is whether we will allow a vocal minority of politicians to weaken our national security with their opposition to missile defense. I am one American who hopes missile defense will finally receive the long-term commitment it deserves—and that we, as Americans, deserve.

At some point, all Americans will be sufficiently motivated to prepare for, and defend against missile attack. The only question is when will we become motivated? Will it be in time to prevent the attack? Or the day after? The answer to these questions will shape history and change our lives in ways we can only imagine.

On September 10, 2001, few Americans were focused on the threat of terrorism even though it was real and about to reveal itself. By mid-morning on September 11th, we all had become very focused. Will we repeat this error?

We could have avoided the devastation of September 11th had the leaders of the 1990s accepted George Washington's advice to obtain peace and security through preparation and strength. Unfortunately, for most of the 1990s, the White House could not muster any real or sustained interest in preparing America's defense against terrorism or missile attack. As a result, Americans witnessed in 1992 terrorists bomb the World Trade Center, killing six and wounding scores of others in an unsuccessful attempt to topple the towers with trucks loaded with explosives. This was treated as a run-of-the-mill crime, but not as a national security threat. As a result, the perpetrator sits in a prison cell, but the terrorist cells that planned and organized the attacks continued their plans and struck again almost nine years later.

Later in 1993, warlords killed 28 American soldiers and wounded 133 others who had been sent to keep the peace and distribute food to a war-ravaged Somalia. On October 4, 1993 mobs desecrated the bodies of three American soldiers who been killed and dragged their bodies through the streets of Mogadishu.

In 1998, we saw terrorists bomb and level two of our embassies in Kenya and Tanzania, killing 257 people and wounding over 5,000. In 2000, terrorist cells bombed the U.S.S. Cole, killing 17 sailors and nearly sinking the ship while it refueled. The White House denounced these attacks in the press, but did little else. As a result, our enemies became emboldened and stronger and we became comparatively weaker and less prepared.

The weakness America projected during most of the 1990s came home to roost on September 11, 2001. Great harm is done when we communicate to our enemies that we are not prepared or willing to defend ourselves.

The question is whether we will repeat this mistake. Will some politicians continue to make missile defense a third-tier priority—or worse yet, openly oppose it? Will we have the wisdom to focus here and now on the need to defend ourselves from missile attacks? Or will it take a missile attack to wake us up and focus our efforts?

Let's hope the vocal minority in Congress can set aside its lust for pork and its desire to fight President Bush on every point. We simply cannot afford to wake up one morning and have the events of the day force us to focus us on the need for missile defense. At that point, it would be too little, too late.

George Washington did not know anything about missiles or missile interceptors, but he would have known exactly what we must do because he understood that "to be prepared for war is one of the most effectual means of preserving peace." Let's hope Congress is listening.

Stumbling Over the Truth

(Originally published in August 2003)

Winston Churchill once said, "Men occasionally stumble over the truth, but most of them pick themselves up and hurry off as if nothing ever happened." Churchill was not speaking of national security or missile defense, but his words apply nonetheless. The truth is the United States currently has no defense against a missile attack. If terrorists or a rogue nation launched a missile attack, we could not protect ourselves.

The threat is serious, real and growing. Terrorists are searching feverishly for missiles to buy or for the parts to construct their own. North Korea is resuming its nuclear program and already has missiles that can reach the United States. During the last decade, China significantly upgraded their offensive missile capability by stealing U.S. technology. Iran has a growing missile capacity and is aggressively seeking more technology.

Some congressional "leaders" stumble over these facts and nonetheless dust themselves off and scurry away. Some oppose President Bush's plan to develop and deploy a robust, multilayered missile defense system. They make a number of claims——that missile defense is unproved and cannot work, that it is too expensive and that it will divert us from the war on terror. Each of these claims is false. But their frequent repetition lends imagined credibility nonetheless. If we ignore the truth after stumbling over it, we do so at our own peril.

Detractors say it cannot be done—"You cannot shoot down a 'bullet' with another 'bullet.'" They are wrong. Four of the last five tests were successful. The only recent test shortcoming was caused when the booster rocket did not properly separate. That is a simple quality-control issue—not a weakness of the technology.

These tests are no easy feats. The interceptor first locates and pursues the missile. Then it distinguishes the missile from decoys. Finally, at a closing speed in excess of 15,000 miles per hour (twenty times the speed of sound), it slams into the missile, destroying it in a "body-to-body" collision. Four of the last five tests were successful.

How can anyone say that it can't be done? This is like someone telling Orville and Wilbur Wright that man will never fly *after* they successfully tested their airplane at Kitty Hawk. Was their first flight perfect? No. But the first flight proved it could be done and opened the way to great improvements. Likewise, current missile defense tests prove we can shield ourselves from missiles.

Detractors also complain that missile defense will cost too much. However, missile defense is a bargain. How much would we have been willing to pay to avoid the events of September 11th? Without even attempting to put a price on the lives lost on September 11th, the economic costs alone have exceeded hundreds of billions of dollars. In the coming years, if America suffers a missile attack, it will be much worse than September 11th. Those who say missile defense costs too much are not considering the alternative.

Detractors also claim that missile defense will distract us from the war on terror. However, missile defense is a *key part* of the war on terror. To say that testing and deploying a missile defense system will divert us from the war on terror is like saying developing and building the best tanks or armored-personnel carriers will divert us from the war on terror. Having the best possible equipment for our fighting men and women is critical to our war on terror. Likewise, having the ability to defend ourselves from missile attack is a critical part of our homeland defense and the war on terror.

President George W. Bush has announced that by the end of 2004 or early 2005, we will have ten land-based missile interceptors. By 2006, we will add ten more interceptors. Critics will argue that the system is not yet perfect. But this initial step will give Americans significant protection from missile attack. Moreover, it will be the foundation for future, more sophisticated missile defenses. President Bush's aim is to shield Americans from the threat of missile attack. It is time for the detractors to stop stumbling over the truth and pretending nothing happened.

Our Generation's Day of Infamy

(Originally published in September 2001)

Like most Americans, I went to work on Tuesday, September 11, 2001 thinking it would be a normal, busy workday. It never occurred to me that America would endure the most serious attack on its soil since 1812. We will all remember this day—September 11th—as a day of infamy, a day of lost innocence and as a day of profound shock, sorrow and anger.

The greatest nation the world has known, history's most awesome economic and military power, was attacked by a group of cowardly and evil men. This group of craven zealots inflicted more damage on American soil in roughly three hours than Hitler's Germany, Mussolini's Italy, Hirohito's Japan and the Soviet Union—combined. It was war on American soil.

Newscasters said throughout the day that the world had changed. We all understand what they meant, but the world had not changed. What changed was our understanding and realization of the dangers posed by our enemies. On September 10th, the world was a dangerous place. We had enemies who meant us harm. There were planes that could be hijacked and flown into buildings. There were those who were willing to do it. We did not believe what happened on September 11th was possible. The problem was, before September 11th, we did not fully realize these facts. Now we do. We've seen it. We watched it happen with shock, horror, sadness and now righteous indignation and anger.

There is much to be done. There are victims and survivors and their families to comfort, heroes and loved ones to be honored and remembered, lives and buildings to be rebuilt and prayers to be offered. But there is also the important task of making sure this *never* happens again.

First, we must harshly punish all those who are involved in terrorism. It will not be enough to simply punish those directly involved in this most recent attack. Any person, group, organization or nation that is involved with, supports, aids, facilitates or harbors terrorists must be targeted for harsh punishment. We should treat them as an opposing and menacing army in need of annihilation, not as common street thugs in need of arrest. A staggering cost must be imposed on anyone and any government that is in any way involved in terrorism.

Second, we must retool and retrain our military and our intelligence services so that we can protect our nation from this new threat. At every phase of our nation's existence, we have developed the military and weapons and intelligence to protect us from our enemies. We must build the military strength and intelligence-gathering capacity to stop future attacks and to exterminate terrorists before they attack next.

We must develop a defense against a wide array of potential attacks. Simply increasing airport security, for example, will not do the job. Our attackers will simply try something else—and almost assuredly something more deadly. For this reason, we must deploy a missile defense system. Naysayers argue that terrorists don't need missiles—they can use airliners. But to argue that we should not defend ourselves from missile attacks because this time the attackers used jetliners is just as absurd as saying that police departments should not buy bulletproof vests for their officers because not all deaths can be prevented by their use.

The events of September 11th show that terrorists are sophisticated and organized and will attack us with whatever works. If we are vulnerable to missile attack, they will attack us with missiles. If we do not build a missile defense, sooner or later, they will attack us with missiles. And when they do, the blood of the victims will be on the hands of those leaders who prevented America from protecting itself.

There are those who argue against increased spending on national defense, that we cannot afford missile defense and that we have more important things to do with that money. Anyone who says these things after seeing the events of September 11th is simply not paying attention to the lessons of history. In words that have new relevance, the American patriot Samuel Adams said to those who challenged the necessity of the American Revolution, "If ye love wealth better than liberty, the tranquility of servitude better than the animating contest of freedom, go home from us in peace. We ask not your counsels or arms. Crouch down and lick the hands which feed you. May your chains set lightly upon you, and may posterity forget that ye were our countrymen."

Third, we must avoid the temptation to achieve security by sacrificing our freedom. Protecting our national security is critically important, but we must not sacrifice our constitutional freedoms in the process. Benjamin Franklin correctly observed, "They that can give up essential liberty to obtain a little temporary safety deserve neither liberty nor safety."

If we learn nothing else from the events of September 11th, let us learn that we must be fully committed to protecting our nation and our citizens because we have enemies who are committed to our destruction. Let us pray we rise to the challenge.

American Security and Energy After 9/11

(Originally published in October 2001)

America has a heavy heart as it honors the lost. President George W. Bush, said it well, "We will read all these names. We will linger over them, and learn their stories, and America will weep." It is right that we should mourn and honor the lost.

But it is also right that we should plan and strengthen our nation so that we do not witness a repeat of this horror. We will undoubtedly see tighter security at airports. We will beef-up our intelligence efforts. We have and must maintain a strong and well-trained military. We must have a defense against missiles to avoid future and even more devastating attacks. And we must hunt down terrorists and those that aid them.

All of these goals are important and worthy of our support. But, we must also reevaluate our energy policy. Today, America obtains nearly two-thirds of its oil from foreign sources. We are now more dependent than at any other time in our history upon potentially unstable and unfriendly sources for our energy.

Our dependence on foreign oil is particularly unsettling because as America works to eradicate terrorism, there will likely be considerable instability in the Middle East. Such instability may make our energy sources even more unreliable. Without reliable energy at stable prices, America's economy may falter.

This is not the time to be so dependent on Middle East oil. This is not to say America should not proceed with its plans to eradicate terrorism. Let there be no mistake, we have a duty to our nation and our posterity to secure the blessings of liberty. But, we must understand that our current dependence on foreign oil does not make America safer, stronger or more secure. This must change.

We need an energy policy that will reduce our dependence on foreign oil, that permits us to explore and produce oil domestically and that will ensure the availability and stable prices of energy. We must stop pursuing harmful international treaties—like the Kyoto Protocol—that would reduce our national security, place America at an economic disadvantage and sharply increase our energy costs—while providing no real environmental benefit.

We must stop allowing radical environmentalists to impose their extremist and destructive agenda on us. America has rich energy reserves that the extreme environmental left has successfully prevented us from using. We simply cannot afford to be so dependent on foreign energy sources—particularly not at this time.

All Americans want to protect the environment. But we also want to protect our nation, our liberty and our way of life. New technologies permit us to explore and extract energy without damaging the environment. Simply stated, we do not have to choose between a healthy environment and a free and prosperous nation. We can have both. We must demand both.

So, where can we find such an energy policy? This past spring, President Bush outlined a bold, new energy policy aimed at reducing America's dependence on foreign oil, increasing the availability of all forms of energy, maintaining price stability and protecting the environment.

The president's proposal included allowing exploration and drilling offshore and in ANWR (Arctic National Wildlife Refuge). The hard left fiercely attacked the president's proposal. Their rhetoric was harsh. They misrepresented the facts. They gravely warned that oil production in Alaska would destroy the pristine environment. But, here are the real facts. The total footprint for drilling in ANWR would be less than two thousand acres out of almost 20 million acres—the equivalent of a postage stamp on a football field. Those two thousand acres are buried under a sheet of ice most of the year and there are no trees.

Many groups supported the president's proposal, but the hard left lined up to oppose it. They received lots of media attention and, at least temporarily, sidetracked the president's much needed energy policy.

Perhaps, they felt they had the luxury of opposing a sensible energy policy last spring. But, it has now become all too obvious that we no longer enjoy such luxury. We are at a crossroads. We can either support America's energy and national security strength or we can support America's continued dependence.

For the sake of our liberty and security, I hope we have the courage to stand up against those that would use the environment as an excuse to betray our national security, our economic strength and our national interests.

Diplomacy without Power is like Praying to an Idol

(Originally published in November 2001)

While the vast majority of Americans strongly support the war against terrorism, there are those vocal few who argue against any use of military power and say that we should make a greater attempt at diplomacy. This small, but noisy anti-war crowd seem to fall into one of two camps—either they believe the use of force is immoral and will only encourage more violence or they believe the use of force makes the United States look bad, like a high-tech bully. Both camps seem to miss a basic and undeniable truth—diplomacy without power is no better than praying to an idol.

Dictators and totalitarian regimes do not respond to the power of moral suasion. Despots simply do not respect morality or the value of well-reasoned arguments. They only understand power and the threat of force. Power is the universal language.

Without power—both economic and military—to back it up, diplomacy is a useless tool. However, with military and economic might backing it up, diplomacy becomes a highly effective means to protect our national interests.

To hear the anti-war crowd tell it, we simply need more understanding and common ground with our enemies. If that were true, we could have avoided the death and destruction of World War II by simply having a rational conversation with Adolph Hitler. Imagine trying to reason with Hitler that the slaughter of six million Jews is immoral or that his occupation of Europe denied millions of their basic human rights. Only the most delusional among us could believe this approach would have worked.

The fact is Hitler responded to one thing—military force. All the talking in the world would not deter him. But superior forces on the sea and land and in the air spoke loudly to him. Our military might spoke with such clarity and loudness, that Hitler finally took his own life—presumably because he did not like was he was hearing.

Let us examine an illustrative hypothetical. Suppose you met an anti-war protester who told you that while the attacks of September 11th were horrific, our military response is immoral and that it will only encourage more violence. What would happen if you punched the protester in the nose as hard as you could? He would probably get up from the ground angry, perhaps ready to punch you back. Then suppose you told this peacenik that he cannot defeat violence with more violence. You then suggest that your differences be worked out peaceably. Now let us assume that as soon as the peacenik agrees, you punch him in the nose again—only harder this time. He gets up off the ground even more angry and is ready to fight, but you begin to remind him that violence is against everything he stands for and that more violence will only beget more violence. How many more times will it take before this silly peacenik realizes that until he stops you, you are going to continue punching him?

This is the lesson that the anti-war crowd simply does not understand—we must stop those who mean to destroy us. Moreover, using force to stop violence and protect freedom is moral. Refusing to stop the aggressor is immoral.

Strength does not beget violence. Strength promotes peace. Weakness invites violence.

So why do terrorists attack the United States? In most cases, it is because they believe we will not respond to their attacks. Since the end of the Gulf War, we have given terrorists every reason to believe there will be little or no price to be paid for attacking America.

In 1993, they tried to blow-up the World Trade Center and we treated it like an ordinary liquor store robbery. In 1993, they killed twenty American soldiers in Somalia who were providing food to the starving population. The terrorists dragged the bodies of our soldiers through the streets. We did nothing. In 1996, they bombed a U.S. military barracks in Saudi Arabia killing nineteen Americans. Again, we did nothing.

In 1998, they blew up two of our embassies in Africa, killing 223 people. We launched a few cruise missiles into the desert, largely for political reasons, but did nothing else. In 2000, they attacked the U.S.S. Cole, killing seventeen sailors. We again did nothing. For most of the 1990s, we exhibited weakness. Over that time, terrorists grew more and more confident that we simply would not react to their atrocities.

During the 1990s, we fell victim to the anti-war crowd's delusional belief that strength in defense of liberty will lead to more violence. The anti-war crowd could not have been more mistaken. Imagine how different things might have been on September 11th, if during the 1990s, we actually had refused to tolerate terrorist attacks and had used our military might to stop terrorism wherever it was found.

George Washington said, "To be prepared for war is one of the most effectual means of preserving peace." George Washington was right and the anti-war crowd needs to go back and study history.

Looking to the Heavens for High Ground

(Originally published in November 2001)

After the events of September 11th, national security has taken on a whole new meaning. In the pre-September 11th world, being the world superpower meant we did not have to worry about attacks on our soil from foreign enemies. In the post-September world, we know that as few as nineteen hateful cowards can kill thousands, cause devastating damage and disrupt the nation's economy.

From the White House and Congress all the way down to local law enforcement, we have begun to re-evaluate security. In the post-September 11th world, it is obvious that airport security must be improved. But we must seriously reexamine the less obvious. Let us remember that on September 10th, it was not obvious that our airport security was woefully inadequate. We must do more than fix the obvious.

Are we seriously examining how our enemies might try to disable our technological and military advantages? Are we shoring up our defenses against some of the most serious threats to our national security? To find the answer, just look to the heavens. The answer for now is no.

What would we do if our enemies disabled or destroyed key satellites? How would our troops communicate? How would our military jets complete precision missions? How would we defend ourselves if our military were temporarily blind? The fact is if our key satellites were inoperable or disabled, the huge technological advantage we enjoy would be largely eliminated. Our fighting men and women would be at greater risk and our national security would be at greater risk.

But that is not all! How would commerce go forward? If the collapse of two towers and the partial destruction of the Pentagon can send world markets into the worst week in Wall Street's history, imagine what would happen if all satellite communications were knocked out. This would be an economic nightmare.

This is not at far-out or hysterical concern. Immediately before becoming Secretary of Defense, Donald Rumsfeld chaired the "Space Commission" organized by Congress to assess the risk to our space-based communications and military assets and to suggest a course of action to avoid a rendezvous with that risk. The risk is real. If we do not begin to protect ourselves, we will one day wake up and realize that we should have prepared. But then it will be too late. The time of preparation will have passed.

The fact is for a few thousand dollars our enemies can buy rather simple electronic components that can temporarily disable our satellites. For a little more money, they can render our satellites essentially useless. To be sure, if our enemies are capable of planning the attacks of September 11th, they are capable of planning this sort of attack. In many respects, an attack against our satellites would be easier to coordinate and execute. Even on September 11th, our airports had some security measures in place. Today our satellites have virtually no security in place.

Our space capabilities are increasingly attractive targets for hostile actions against the United States. As we have so vividly witnessed, threats to our security can come from small nations, groups or even individuals. The ability to deny, disrupt or physically destroy space systems and the ground facilities that use and control them are available on the open market and sold to the highest bidder.

The Navy defends its aircraft carriers. The Air Force defends its airfields. The Army defends its bases. But we do not defend one of our greatest military assets—our satellites. It is time to get our defenses up so that in some not too distant day, we don't wake up feeling even more vulnerable than we did on September 11th.

The security of the United States depends on our ability to operate successfully in space. It is far easier and a great strategic advantage to defend from higher ground. We must begin looking at space as the next "high ground."

ABM Treaty: Doing the Right Thing

(Originally published in January 2002)

About a month ago, President George W. Bush stood outside the White House in the Rose Garden to announce that the United States would exercise its right under the 1972 Anti-Ballistic Missile Treaty (ABM) to give six months notice of our intent to withdraw from the treaty. Detractors and disciples of arms control immediately warned that this would destabilize relations with Russia and cause another arms race. In the month that has passed since that day, it has become clear that these naysayers were wrong. What has been remarkable is that Russia hardly seems to care. There have been no dire consequences of pursuing a policy that will protect Americans from missile attacks. Even the Russians understood that our withdrawal from the ABM treaty was inevitable, appropriate and warranted.

To those who have implied we "broke" the ABM Treaty, the answer is simple—the Treaty itself explicitly provides that a nation may withdraw from it by giving six months notice to the parties of the treaty. President Bush simply exercised this option. Thus, everything was done in accordance with the terms of the treaty.

The truth is that President Bush's action made the United States a safer more secure place. Why? Because the ABM Treaty prohibited the United States from building a missile defense. Most Americans believe that the United States has a missile defense system. But we don't. Thanks to President Ronald Reagan and now President Bush, we have been working to develop a missile defense system. But the ABM Treaty prohibited testing beyond certain minimal levels and strictly prohibits deployment of a national missile defense system.

Under the ABM Treaty, our only defense against a missile attack was to promise to fire a missile back at the attacking nation. This was appropriately named Mutually Assured Destruction (MAD). While I have trouble with the notion that we purposefully chose not to defend ourselves and chose only to visit our enemies with an equally devastating blow, one could argue that as between two superpowers like the United States and the Soviet Union such threats of retaliation might deter a missile attack.

However, the world looks very different today. The Soviet Union no longer exists. Our primary threat today is not an enemy with borders and large conventional armies, but a cowardly enemy that hides throughout the world and ventures out only long enough to visit death and destruction on innocent civilians. Then it goes back into hiding to wait for another opportunity to kill and destroy.

We now know that these terrorists have been trying to obtain missile, chemical, biological and nuclear capabilities for some time. There is reason to believe that they have received help from a few rogue nations. It is all too obvious that MAD will not prevent future missile attacks from the sorts of zealots who planned and perpetrated the attacks of September 11th.

If these cowardly foes were to launch a missile at the United States and were to kill tens of thousands of Americans, MAD would do us little service and provide no protection. Where would we launch our retaliatory missiles? We would be left hoping to find the perpetrators while we mourned our dead and rebuilt our cities.

President Bush's vision and mission are sound—to defend this nation and its people, to prevent any attack we possibly can, and to hunt down any attackers as we are doing with the al Qaeda and the Taliban in Afghanistan.

The day President Bush announced our withdrawal from the ABM treaty, I had the opportunity to meet with him briefly. He looked me and my companions in the eye and explained that he will not leave our defense to chance. He made it crystal clear that he would not be deterred from protecting this nation or from hunting down those responsible for attacking America.

There were no reporters in the room. He was not posturing. He was making a simple and direct declaration of his vision and mission. As I listened, I was grateful for a president who speaks with clarity and strength of purpose and who understands the moral imperative to defend our citizens and our homeland. Best of all, I have confidence that he meant every word of it.

Ditching ABM and Protecting America

(Orginally published in June 2002)

On December 13, 2001, the United States gave the required six months notice that it intended to withdraw from the Anti-Ballistic Missile Treaty (ABM). Now, six months later, the United States stands poised to officially withdraw from the ABM Treaty. This is good news for the United States and for Americans who want security from missile attack. Here's why—the ABM Treaty prevented America from building a missile defense and instead relied on retaliation as the only protection against attack.

Contrary to popular misconception, the ABM Treaty provided no real protection against missile attack. It simply limited both the United States and the Soviet Union to a set number of missiles and warheads—a large enough number to destroy most everything in both countries. Experts can argue whether these limits were a good or a bad thing. However, no one can seriously disagree that the ABM Treaty prohibited the United States from defending itself from missile attack.

If our enemies launched missiles to flatten our cities and kill millions of our citizens, we could not destroy the incoming missiles. Currently, we do not have a defensive shield to stop the missiles. All we could do is let the missiles hit their targets, level our cities and kill our people. Then we could retaliate and level their cities and kill their people. That is cold comfort.

I am much more interested in stopping incoming missiles and protecting American lives—yours and mine and our family's and neighbor's—than I am in killing an equal number of their citizens or leveling an equal number of their cities. Once we are vaporized in a mushroom cloud, we would find little vindication and even less solace in the fact that somewhere in the world our enemies were about to suffer a similar fate.

Here is a bold proposal—perhaps we should stop our enemies from killing us and leveling our cities. Perhaps we should build a defense so that they cannot destroy our cities or kill us. Perhaps having the ability to prevent the attack would be more effective than sitting back and waiting for the attack to come while promising to return the favor.

This is precisely what President George W. Bush has said he will do—build a missile defense. Yet, detractors complain that it is a bad idea and unnecessary. Despite the naysayers, President Bush has moved forward to protect America just as he promised. He has steadfastly made the point that America will be safer only if it can actually defend itself against attack.

The logic of this is irrefutable and inescapable. Does it make more sense to keep thieves out by locking the front door while you're away or to leave the door wide open and post a sign that says, "If you rob me, I'll rob you." There is a reason why hardware stores sell locks, but don't sell signs threatening retaliation for robbery. Locked doors work. They may not prevent all crime, but they substantially reduce it. I doubt threats of retaliatory robbery would make much difference at all.

The same is true of missiles. A robust missile defense is like a locked door. It will stop missile attacks. Likewise, a threat of retaliation won't stop most enemies—certainly not terrorists or madmen despots like Saddam Hussein.

Either we prepare to stop their attacks or eventually we will witness a repeat of September 11th. Next time it will be worse because it will be real missiles with real warheads, not passenger planes loaded with fuel.

President Bush understands the moral imperative to protect America from attack. It simply does not matter what else the government does well, if it cannot protect its citizens. Since the ABM Treaty was preventing America from protecting itself, President Bush courageously and correctly decided that the ABM Treaty must go.

Fortunately, the treaty itself permits the United States to withdraw after giving six months notice, which was done last December. With six months having passed, the United States will officially withdrawal from the treaty and can move forward with an effective missile defense.

Naysayers who are in bondage to the arms-control dogma of the past will reflexively criticize President Bush's leadership. However, those who can see and understand reality, realize that the world is a better and safer place when the United States can protect itself by stopping incoming missiles.

Democrats Vote to Keep America Beholden to Saddam

(Originally published in April 2002)

Democrats in the U.S. Senate blocked the cornerstone of President George W. Bush's plan to make America more energy secure and less dependent on foreign oil. As a result, America will continue to import most of its oil from the volatile and hostile Middle East. Simply stated, Senators Tom Daschle, John Kerry and Joe Lieberman led the charge in the U.S. Senate to make sure that America grows ever more dependent upon folks like Saddam Hussein for our energy.

The whole point of the Bush energy plan was to make sure that terrorist states could not hold us hostage with their oil. But the Democratic leadership in the Senate doesn't think we need more of our own energy. Their plan was to legislate that Americans drive smaller cars. Since we import 57% of our oil, we are left to assume that they wanted us to drive 57% less or drive cars that are 57% smaller. That goofy plan does not even pass the "straight-face test."

For the last two or more decades, extreme environmentalists have tried to prevent energy exploration and extraction on U.S. soil. As a result, we have become more and more dependent on hostile and unstable sources for oil. Unfortunately, most Senate Democrats are beholden to these environmental extremists. As a result, American policy of the last 25 or more years has perpetuated and exacerbated our dependence on foreign energy and forced America's economy to rely upon unstable sources for its energy needs.

Democrats defend their vote to keep America dependent on Middle East oil by claiming that drilling in Alaska will "destroy the environment." They also claim that drilling will not generate enough oil to make any real difference. They are wrong on both counts.

In 1960, during the Eisenhower administration, the Alaska National Wildlife Range was established with about 9 million acres being set aside. About twenty years later, President Jimmy Carter and the Democrat-controlled Congress went a step further and created the Arctic National Wildlife Refuge (ANWR) and more than doubled its original size to almost 20 million acres. Because of the Organization of the Petroleum Exporting Countries (OPEC) oil embargo and the need to have more domestic energy, the Carter administration and the Democratic-controlled Congress set aside an area of ANWR *specifically* for oil and gas exploration. It is in this area that was specifically set aside for oil exploration that President Bush proposed drilling.

Alaska is a state of 365 million acres. ANWR is almost 20 million acres, the size of the state of South Carolina. The proposed drilling site in ANWR would be less than 2000 acres—less than one-hundredth of one percent of ANWR. Denver International Airport is 17 times *larger* than the proposed drilling site in ANWR. Drilling on such a small site cannot possibly destroy the environment—particularly given the new technologies that would be used to preserve and safeguard the environment.

If the State of Alaska were a regulation-sized football field, the drilling site in ANWR would be a little larger than a postage stamp. Put another way, if Alaska were a two-hour movie, the drilling site in ANWR would be less than four one-hundredths of a second—literally the blink of an eye.

Experts estimate that ANWR contains up to 16 billion barrels of oil. It would take the United States 30 years at our current import levels to buy that much oil from Saudi Arabia. ANWR alone could produce 10% of our daily oil needs. While ANWR by itself, will not solve all of our energy needs, it would be a strong first step to helping America become less dependent on foreign oil. It would show the world, and most importantly, our enemies, that we will not allow anyone to hold us hostage over oil.

What message have Senators Daschle, Kerry and their friends sent to our enemies? That America is content to give unstable and even hostile nations the means to hold us hostage. That we would rather send our young men and women to die in battle to protect our oil interests in far away lands, than drill on a small portion of frozen tundra in Alaska. With "leaders" and "statesmen" like Daschle and Kerry, who needs enemies?

National Security, CAFE and Other Tales

(Originally published in January 2003)

Beware of snake oil salesmen and those who champion more stringent energy regulations as a way to finally make us more secure and reduce our dependence on foreign oil. Throughout the 1970s we tried that tactic and it did not work. In fact, despite all the energy regulations imposed—or perhaps because of them—we are now more dependent on foreign oil than ever before.

Senators Tom Daschle and John Kerry and their allies in the U.S. Senate have begun to suggest that rather than developing more of our own energy here in the United States, we should mandate smaller, lighter cars for everyone. They don't like minivans or trucks and they hate SUVs—unless, of course, they get to drive in them.

They tell us that by further increasing CAFE standards (Corporate Average Fuel Economy), we will use less oil and, therefore, not be dependent on foreign sources. To the casual observer this may sound reasonable, but to anyone who has followed the history of CAFE regulations and their consequences, such talk is just plain silly and without merit.

The Energy Policy & Conservation Act of 1975 created CAFE regulations. The stated purpose of the Act and of CAFE regulations was twofold—to increase energy conservation and to reduce our reliance on foreign or imported oil. The fact is CAFE has failed on both counts. In 1974, the United States imported about one-third of its oil from foreign sources. Today, twenty-seven years later, we import almost 60% of our oil. That is almost double.

CAFE regulations have increased mileage averages substantially—from 18 miles per gallon in 1978 to 27.5 miles per gallon now. However, our oil consumption has increased, not decreased. We can now afford more cars and larger cars. We commute longer distances. CAFE regulations have *not* done what they were supposed to do.

But CAFE regulations have not been without effect. Highway experts agree that CAFE regulations are responsible for over 2,000 highway deaths each year and even more serious injuries because cars are made lighter to meet the mileage requirements. Moreover, CAFE regulations have added about $2,750 to the sticker price of the average car so that families have a harder time buying new, cleaner burning automobiles and drive older cars that pollute more. Moreover, our pollution laws are written so that regardless of the mileage of a car, it must meet the same stringent clean air standards. Thus, a huge SUV cannot put out any more emissions than an econobox car.

The bottom line is that CAFE has no upside and plenty of downside—increased highway deaths and injury, higher sticker prices for new cars, more pollution and as we've seen for over twenty-five years, a greater dependence on foreign oil. None of this will promote our national security.

So why are Daschle, Kerry and company promoting CAFE as a national security issue? The answer is simple. They oppose every measure that President George W. Bush and Vice President Richard Cheney have put forth to improve our energy national security. Senators Daschle and Kerry are simply looking for an issue to hide this unpleasant fact.

For example, Senator Daschle has refused to even allow the Senate to seriously debate oil exploration in Alaska. These folks also oppose allowing the use of new technologies which are environmentally friendly in offshore exploration.

In addition to encouraging conservation, the administration's proposal would open federal lands to exploration—but with stringent environmental safeguards. Additionally, the proposal would limit drilling to just 2,000 acres—a relative flyspeck in the 19.6 million-acre barren refuge that few Americans have seen or will ever see. Since September 11th, Americans in numerous national polls have agreed with the administration's plan to move forward with drilling in the Arctic refuge because the facts clearly show that the positives far outweigh the negatives.

But for Daschle, Kerry and company this is simply not enough. They want to solve our energy needs by forcing us to use 60% less energy. That cannot be done given current technologies. Using 60% less energy would mean that we drive 60% less, we heat and cool our homes 60% less, that we have 60% fewer jobs and that we have 60% less income.

Conservation is important. For about thirty years, that's been our focus—conserve, converse, conserve. We should continue the effort to conserve and increase efficiency. But we cannot conserve ourselves into a strong economy or a nation secure from enemies. We must also focus on obtaining more domestic energy sources.

When Daschle, Kerry and company suggest that what we need is more CAFE regulations, don't forget that we've been trying this prescription for over twenty-five years and it has not worked. It is time to try something that works—like responsibly developing our own energy sources so that other nations cannot hold us hostage with energy. Energy security is part of national security. It is time for Daschle, Kerry and their allies to stop playing politics with our nation's vital interests.

Old Europe vs. New Europe

(Originally published in February 2003)

France and Germany, a.k.a. Old Europe, oppose U.S. plans to disarm Saddam Hussein's Iraq. After twelve years of breaking treaties and disregarding seventeen UN resolutions, Saddam steadfastly refuses to disarm and continues to play cat and mouse games. Old Europe believes still more time, talk and inspections are needed. However, most of Europe, including former Soviet-block nations, support the U.S. position. New Europe understands that Saddam will not voluntarily disarm.

So why this disagreement? The divide has many causes, including: (i) Old Europe's power and prestige are declining which they bitterly resent, (ii) Old Europe has a long history of appeasement which they call giving peace a chance but which history proves only gives tyranny a chance, and (iii) New Europe remembers Soviet domination and who helped them escape it.

First, France and Germany, once great nations, are now second-rate economic and military powers. The world does not look to them for leadership. Their best days are past. They resent this fact and attempt to throw around weight they simply do not have—hoping to convince the world and themselves that they are still powerful. However, as more and more nations side with America, they are forced to face their own impotence. This only angers them more.

For example, France's Jacques Chirac lashed out at European nations siding with America—calling them "infantile," and "badly brought up," and saying "they had missed a good opportunity to shut-up." His tirade ended with a threat to block their admission to the European Union.

Perhaps Mr. Chirac was trying to convince the world community that *he* is infantile or that *he* was badly brought up or that *he* has missed a good opportunity to shut-up . If so, it was a compelling presentation. Chirac's outburst was ugly and it showed France's frustration with being a has-been.

Second, Old Europe's line—that "war is always a sign of failure" and that we need to "give peace a chance"—is the same tripe that French diplomats spewed before World War II. As Hitler's Germany broke disarmament treaties and expanded its borders across Europe, France, among others, wanted to talk and talk.

As a result, Germany occupied most of Europe, including France, before the appeasers realized that giving "peace a chance" was killing Europe. In June 1944,

France, who barely offered any opposition to the Nazi invasion, waited on America and England to liberate them from German occupation. For that moment, France ceased talk of giving peace a chance. Unfortunately, they are back at it now.

How has France forgotten history? Unless France speaks its appeasement arguments in perfect German, we ought not take them seriously. They speak French today because America and England made staggering sacrifices to liberate France.

Third, New Europe remembers the horrors of communism and who steadfastly and actively opposed it. They know why the iron curtain fell. They know why they are now bourgeoning democracies—because America took a principled, but unpopular stand. France and Germany, among others, mocked America. They called Ronald Reagan a renegade cowboy, as they now speak of George Bush. But history proved America right. New Europe remembers history better than Old Europe.

New Europe is also a good bit more grateful. When Charles de Gaulle said that American military bases were no longer welcome in France, President Johnson asked if the French would also like America to remove her war dead. The discussion ended.

Latvian newspaper, *Neatkariga Rita Avize*, expressed the point well, "Perhaps we are poor. Perhaps we were not raised properly. We do not know about wine and…avant-garde art. But we do not repay those who have helped us and continue to help us with ingratitude."

There is a good reason Old Europe is no longer a great power—there has been a consistent failure of leadership that has placed expediency over principle. Conversely, America is great and powerful because she stands for principle even when it is difficult and costly and even when has-beens mock her for doing what is right.

The United Nations is Rapidly Making Itself Irrelevant

(Originally published in April 2003)

The United Nations is in the process of making itself irrelevant. It has spent the last twelve years drawing lines in the sand and telling Iraq's Saddam Hussein that he had better not cross them. Each time, Saddam crossed the newly drawn line and laughed at the UN. And each time the UN drew a new line, but did nothing about the previous violations.

The fact that the UN's credibility is now on life support does not mean the UN has never accomplished anything or that it cannot achieve something of value in the future. Reform is always possible. The UN may be able to aid refugees or help fight disease in the third world. However, it is not clear that other organizations with similar funding couldn't do better.

But, when it comes to the war on terrorism, the UN is diminishing itself. If the UN continues on its current path, it will write its own obituary. The League of Nations suffered a similar fate some sixty years ago—dying of self-inflicted wounds to its credibility.

The reasons for the UN's lack of credibility are numerous, but three of the most significant factors include: (i) the UN operates on a false premise, (ii) the UN is profoundly confused and rudderless, and (iii) the UN has become a forum for second-rate nations to bash America.

First, the UN operates on the false premise that all nations are equal. However, some nations are outlaws and rogues. Some are upstanding international citizens. And many fall somewhere in between. Yet, the UN pretends that all nations are equal.

For example, the United States recently lost its seat on the UN Human Rights Commission. This UN commission is now chaired by Muammar Gaddafi's Libya—a terrorist nation with a shocking human rights record. This is like asking a Klu Klux Klan Grand Wizard to chair the Equal Opportunity Commission. But to the UN, it is progress.

Second, the UN has become so perplexed by the "complexities" of the war against terrorism that it cannot figure out who to support. The UN says it wants Saddam to disarm. Yet, the UN is unwilling to do anything to further its stated goal.

The UN argues that the inspectors need more time—while ignoring the fact that Saddam only agreed to the inspectors' return because he did not want the

U.S. Armed Forces to return. Saddam is playing the UN for fools as he plays cat and mouse games with inspectors and hopes that the same UN luminaries who thought Libya should head the Human Rights Commission will protect him from accountability and call for more delays.

Third, the UN has become a platform for wannabe nations to denounce the United States and blame the world's problems on America. Worse yet, this anti-American forum is disproportionately paid for by U.S. taxpayers. Almost one-fourth of the UN's general revenues come from the United States. The United States' share of peacekeeping expenses is even higher. The remaining 190 member nations of the UN split the remaining costs.

For this hefty investment, we are treated to the spectacle of Libya, Iraq, North Korea, Iran and others moralizing about America's shortcomings. Yet, the United States is the one stabilizing force for democracy and long-term peace in the world today.

If the UN doesn't fully reform its operations and bolster its credibility, it will suffer a quick death of irrelevancy just as the League of Nations did. Wouldn't it be a strange twist of fate if Saddam's last victory were the demise of the UN?

Transformation Needed at the State Department

(Originally published in May 2003)

The war in Iraq is over. But there remains much to do and much to accomplish before Iraq can be counted as a stable, democratic ally. Nonetheless, let's pause to review what we can learn about our military and diplomatic efforts. The military effort was spectacularly successful. While there is still more to do, the swift and effective dash to Baghdad was stunning and historic. Unfortunately, our diplomatic efforts were ineffectual.

Why the difference? The military accepted President Bush's foreign policy and did its best to implement his goals to better protect America. In contrast, the State Department, as an institution, has mired itself in perpetuating its own bureaucratic agenda and at times actively opposed the president's foreign policy.

Let's get this straight from the start—I am not attacking Colin Powell. Speaking at the UN, he effectively and powerfully made the case for military action against Saddam. It is difficult to imagine that someone else could have spoken with more credibility. Early this year, when Europeans questioned U.S. military action in Iraq as too aggressive, Powell powerfully reminded them that America has sent its sons and daughters to defend freedom all over the world—including Europe—and America has never asked for anything in return "except enough ground to bury" our dead. My criticism is of the *institution* known as the State Department, not the Secretary of State.

The key question is whether the State Department, as an institution, has worked diligently to promote Bush's policy. Taking Powell out of the equation, the answer appears to be a clear and unambiguous no. The State Department is obligated under the law to advance the foreign policy of the president. Yet, State Department officials have openly opposed the president's foreign policy.

It is a matter of public record that high level State Department officials have: (i) publicly criticized those who advocated and supported the war with Iraq including those on the president's errand, (ii) publicly criticized the president's position on North Korea's nuclear blackmail saying that the United States should begin bilateral negotiations, and (iii) publicly defended Iran as a democracy when it clearly is not and despite the fact that President Bush has correctly identified Iran as part of the "axis of evil."

When America's diplomacy efforts should have been in high gear, the State Department did not make the case for America's military action. U.S. Embassies around the world were not actively or enthusiastically presenting America's case against Saddam. Typically, the diplomatic establishment will appear on news and talk programs and write articles to argue in favor of the administration's policy. Yet, the establishment was surprisingly quiet during the debate on Iraq. The White House created its own Office of Global Communications, at least in part, to do the job the State Department should have done.

Once the war began, State Department officials finally became active in working with the media. Unfortunately, they broke their silence not to support Bush's policies, but rather to criticize the battle plan. Thus, about one week into the war, *The Washington Post* and *The New York Times*, using State Department officials as sources, reported that the war was rushed, poorly planned, and bogged down. They claimed the march to Baghdad could take months. All of this proved to be completely false.

Within days, Iraqis and U.S. Marines pulled down statutes of Saddam in downtown Baghdad. Liberated Iraqis danced in the streets. There is still plenty of difficulty ahead. The transition to democracy will not be as easy or smooth as the defeat of Iraq's army. It should be noted that it took years to restore peace, stability and democracy in Germany after World War II. In Iraq, there will be similar challenges. But the fact that there is still more work to do should not prevent us from acknowledging the striking military success.

The military accepted the president's policies and allowed itself to be shaped by the president's vision. That is one major reason the military was so successful. Conversely, the diplomats have resisted transformation and even tried to obstruct the president's policies. As an institution, the State Department was largely unsuccessful in its diplomatic endeavors because it was trying to be unsuccessful.

It is All about Oil and Money—for the French

(Originally published in July 2003)

Jacques Chirac, president of France, has spent the last six months vociferously protecting the Butcher of Baghdad. Saddam Hussein has had no closer ally than Chirac.

Saddam has been defying the 1991 ceasefire agreement for twelve years and flouting seventeen UN resolutions. Saddam has killed and tortured hundreds of thousands of Iraqis to maintain his brutal dictatorship. Saddam has provided safe haven to al Qaeda terrorists.

World leaders all admit that Saddam had weapons of mass destruction. There is proof positive—he killed tens of thousands of Kurds with such weapons. Additionally, UN weapons inspectors found tons of such weapons. The evidence is that Saddam continues to pursue and develop weapons of mass destruction. His own behavior is consistent with someone who has or is seeking these weapons. Intercepted Iraqi communiqués reveal that Saddam has authorized the use of chemical weapons.

Despite this, Chirac has steadfastly said that there are no circumstances under which France would support military action to liberate Iraqis from Saddam's murderous grip. Some European newspapers have taken to calling Chirac "Saddam's whore." This may sound harsh, but it is true.

Fair minded, honest and reasonable people can, in good faith, see things differently. However, Mr. Chirac's differences are not based in honest or good faith differences of opinion. He understands the facts and simply chooses to look the other way to hide his own unseemly blemishes.

Chirac lies as freely as Saddam kills. Chirac accuses the United States of pursing war against Iraq for oil—the tired and discredited "No oil for blood" argument. Yet, Chirac opposed Iraqi's liberation because France wanted to protect its oil contracts and other deals with Saddam's regime. When faced with choosing between supporting the liberation of Iraqis from Saddam's torture, rape and murder and supporting France's oil contracts, Chirac sided with the oil and the money.

Saddam's regime kills its own citizens, uses children as human shields and houses its troops and equipment in schools, hospitals and family neighborhoods while indignantly accusing the United States of harming Iraqi civilians. Likewise, France enters into banned oil contracts and other agreements with Saddam's regime and then accuses the United States of impure motives. Chirac is not simply wrong; he is a loathsome and corrupt leader.

Chirac claimed to be an advocate for peace, yet he is the one who submarined peace and diplomacy and forced war. Saddam gave at least the appearance of cooperation when it appeared that the UN would hold him accountable. The only reason Saddam agreed to allow UN inspectors to return to Iraq was that he did not want the U.S. Armed Forces to return. But once Chirac and the timid French made it clear that they would unilaterally veto any military action, Saddam became emboldened and ceased all cooperation. Thus, war became the only option——thanks to Chirac's unilateral veto threats.

After American and British troops took casualties and Saddam broadcasted disturbing pictures of executed POWs and POW interrogations, Chirac demanded that after Iraq is liberated, the United States must step aside and give the leading role to France and those who opposed Iraq's liberation.

Chirac and the French—who worked actively against Iraq's liberation, who feigned moral grounds for their opposition while hiding and protecting their illegal oil contracts; and who have spent no treasure, split no blood and sacrificed nothing to liberate Iraq—want to push the United States aside and play a leadership role in liberated Iraq. To make matters worse, American troops have been attacked with Russian and French technology that was sent to Saddam in violation of UN resolutions. Why should any nation that opposes Iraqi liberation and supports Saddam play a role in Iraqi's post-liberation development?

Some suggest President Bush and the United States must take the first step to mend fences with the French. This is misguided. It is Chirac that must mend fences. The French are the ones who unilaterally tore down fences in their reckless and illegal pursuit of oil and money. They have broken international law. They have attributed their own deplorable motives to the United States. They have protected Saddam's murderous regime.

The United States should make no gesture that is confused with an apology. We owe no apology. Once French leadership ceases their offensive behavior and offers an apology, the United States can, and will, be magnanimous. Until then, we should give them the cold shoulder.

The Dean Lesson: National Security Matters

(Originally published in February 2004)

In early January, Howard Dean was the clear favorite to win the Democratic presidential nomination. He had double digit leads in the polls both in Iowa and New Hampshire, a strong national organization and record amounts of money. But when the Iowa Caucuses were over, Howard Dean finished a distant third and in New Hampshire, a distant second. The question is what happened?

Howard Dean rose to popularity among hard-left activists by bashing President Bush and the War on Terror. While the population at-large supports, and approves of, President Bush's leadership and how he is conducting the war on terror, the public at-large is not participating in the Democratic primaries. The typical Democratic primary participant is a hard-left liberal. As a result, Howard Dean scored early points by serving up large daily portions of red meat to Bush haters. This translated into early popularity among a select crowd and record donations.

This is where the problem began. In his zeal to win the love and support of the extreme left, he began saying things that demonstrated he lacked both the judgment and the temperament to be the President of the United States. On numerous occasions, he lost his temper on the campaign trail. But that was not his biggest problem. Far more damaging was the fact that he was so vehemently and vociferously anti-war that many Americans, even self-identified liberals who vote in primaries, began to see him as not committed to America's safety and security. That was the beginning of the end for Howard Dean's 2004 campaign.

No one who wishes to be President of the United States can afford to be seen as soft on security and less than committed to the nation's defense. Howard Dean made this fatal mistake.

The most dramatic example of Howard Dean's extreme anti-war rhetoric came after Saddam Hussein's capture. Howard Dean steadfastly argued that Americans were no safer after his capture than they were before. While it is certainly true that Saddam's capture does not alone win the war on terror, it is mind-bogglingly foolish to assert that Americans are *no* safer. American soldiers in Iraq are certainly safer. Those who remain loyal to Saddam have less to fight for now that their leader was captured after giving up without a fight. Others may fight on, but at least some Saddam loyalists will figure that if Saddam wouldn't fight, they don't need to either. Objective data shows that the number of attacks on American troops in Iraq have substantially declined during the two months since Saddam's capture.

American civilians living in the fifty states are also safer. Saddam Hussein personally funded terrorism and had ties with a number of terrorist organizations. Numerous al Qaeda operatives and Osama bin Laden lieutenants have been captured in Iraq. Thus, helping Iraq move towards democracy will promote stability in the Middle East and reduce the strength of terrorists. Saddam's capture was a substantial step towards these ends. This can only make America safer.

Perhaps, Howard Dean did not mean what he said, but he was asked to clarify his statement several times, and he simply refused to back away from his obviously silly statement.

Howard Dean also said that once captured, we must make sure that Osama bin Laden receives a fair trial because we should not prejudge these things. There is no question that everyone, including Osama, deserves a fair trial. But these sorts of loopy statements makes it appear that Howard Dean is more concerned with fair trials for Osama than he is for America's security.

When you combine the Osama and the Saddam statements, most Americans were left to wonder if Dean could muster the same anger for America's sworn enemies (i.e. terrorists) as he did for its current president. Simply put, it is fine to disagree with President Bush, but when President Bush makes you angrier than Osama bin Laden and Saddam Hussein combined, then something is seriously out of whack. Thus began the fall of Howard Dean.

The fact that Howard Dean said stupid things with some frequency was not the real problem—the papers are filled with stupid things said by politicians. The damage was caused when it appeared that Howard Dean was more anti-Bush than he was anti-terrorism, more against the war than he was against those who attacked America on September 11, 2001. Simply put, Howard Dean convinced many of those on the extreme left that making America safe is not a high priority for him. Even liberals, the bedrock of his support, came to the conclusion that Howard Dean does not get it. They began to believe that if Howard Dean were elected President of the United States, Americans would be less secure. Most Americans understand that the Constitution makes the president the commander-in-chief for a reason.

Bill Clinton could get away with being soft on defense, because most Americans did not perceive themselves at risk. But after September 11th, all that changed. Americans now believe that they must have a president who is committed to defeating terrorism. While all of the Democratic candidates with the exception of Sen. Joe Lieberman (D-Conn.), have been competing to see who can most sharply attack the president's leadership on the war on terror, none has been as loud or consistent in his criticism of President Bush and the war as Howard Dean. Thus, the issue that lifted Dean at first is now driving him into the ground.

The lesson Howard Dean's rise and fall teaches is that in today's political environment Americans, regardless of whether they are liberal or conservative or moderate, want a leader who will defend America and make it safe from our enemies to the best of his ability. Howard Dean convinced most folks that he was not interested in that part of the job. The question is whether the new presumptive frontrunner, John Kerry, will eventually suffer similar problems—either in the primaries or in the general election—because of his anti-war rhetoric.

Success and Freedom in Iraq

(Originally published in March 2004)

Shortly after U.S. forces entered Baghdad, Iraqis enjoyed their first taste of freedom after more than three decades of brutality and repression. Within a few months, sovereignty will be turned over to the Iraqis and their interim government. But there will be tough times ahead. Iraq has no tradition of freedom or democracy. Dark forces within Iraq will do whatever they can to derail Iraq's rendezvous with freedom and democracy. But the goal is within sight, which is why the dark forces are fighting so hard.

There are those who question whether Iraq can in the long run enjoy freedom and democracy. While I do not share this pessimism, it is worth noting that it took several years to bring stability and democracy to Germany after World War II. For several years after the war's end, American soldiers and German leaders who were viewed as "collaborators" were killed by angry Nazis. Thus, no one should expect Iraq's transition to democracy to be easy or immediate. That is the bad news.

The good news is that Iraq will experience freedom and democracy if Iraq wants it badly enough. Iraq's success in taking this gift of freedom and turning it into a lasting liberty will be dependent on whether its efforts are firmly based in the following principles.

First, the new Iraqi government must understand that its most basic moral obligation is to defend Iraq and its people, not dominate and terrorize them. Saddam, like all tyrants, created a culture of fear and violence and used his military and secret police to enforce his will. The challenge of the new government will be to break this culture and create a military that defends and a police that operates under the rule of law to maintain order, but not impose a ruler's will.

Second, the new Iraqi government must understand that property rights and economic freedom are the fertile soil in which all other rights grow and thrive. Thus, as important as free speech and press are, economic freedom is even more important because when the people are self-sufficient and do not rely on the government for the necessities of life, they can freely speak out and express their opinions without fear of economic reprisals.

Third, the Iraqis will need to establish a government that has limits and checks upon its powers. History has proven that a government that has all power at its disposal will use that power to its greatest advantage. That is what Hitler did.

That is what Stalin did. That is what Saddam did. Iraq must create a government with sufficient power to defend the nation and maintain the rule of law, but not an all-powerful government that can be easily hijacked by a future despot.

Fourth, Iraq must establish a government that will devote itself to protecting the rights of "Life, Liberty, and the pursuit of Happiness." Free speech, freedom of religion, the freedom to own and control private property and fair trials with due process are foundational elements of any free society. There is no established tradition for these rights in Iraq today, but Iraq's new government must devote itself to protecting these rights.

Fifth, Iraq must establish independent courts that have the duty to faithfully and strictly interpret the law. The courts must provide for the equal treatment of all individuals. Tyrants often subvert the courts first as they consolidate their power. The new government must not view the courts as a tool to impose its will, but rather as a system for society to fairly and equitably resolve disputes and impose criminal penalties on those who have committed crimes.

Sixth, the new government must understand that taxes may be legitimately imposed only to the extent necessary to pay for the essential activities of government. To tax more than this is a form of tyranny and extortion. For decades, Iraqis have been heavily taxed so that Saddam, his sons and the ruling class could live in gold-trimmed palaces. Those who serve in the new government cannot view this service as a ticket to wealth and opulence, but rather as a way to lead a nation that yearns for freedom, prosperity and peace.

Seventh, the new government must resist the temptation to mandate and regulate every facet of business dealings and private life. Over-regulation wastes resources, erodes freedom, diminishes property rights and produces harmful unintended consequences. Iraq cannot afford to erode freedom or waste its resources. It will need every advantage as it establishes a new tradition of freedom and democracy.

Eighth, Iraqi leaders must understand that basic standards of morality and civic virtue are essential to building and maintaining economic strength and freedom. Too often, freedom is thought of in a vacuum. But without the widespread acceptance of civic virtue and basic standards of right and wrong, no society can long endure.

Admittedly, achieving these things will not be easy. But all of the world's great democracies have done this. The fact that it won't be easy does not mean that it cannot be done. Liberating Iraq was not easy. But it was done. Likewise, Iraq can, and I pray will, take the necessary steps to establish itself as a free and prosperous democracy.

5

Media Bias and Liberal Hate Speech

Free Speech: An Endangered Species

(Originally published in January 2001)

In America, few rights are held in as high esteem as the freedom of speech—and rightly so. By protecting the right of free speech, the "marketplace of ideas" can flourish. The best ideas rise to the top and the bad ideas become exposed as such.

In an academic setting, freedom of speech is often referred to as academic freedom, but it is essentially the same principle. Understandably, college professors and administrators jealously guard their freedom of speech and academic freedom. However, all too often, today's academics support free speech for themselves, but find it offensive when practiced by others with whom they disagree.

There is a disturbing trend in academia. Colleges all across America have revoked student funding for conservative publications while maintaining funding for more liberal publications. College administrators have zealously defended the right of liberal students to steal thousands of conservative student newspapers from kiosks simply because the liberal students did not like what they read and wanted to prevent others from reading. Conservative student groups have been forced to jump through onerous administrative hoops to obtain approval or funding for activities. Expressing opinions—particularly conservative ones—can bring disciplinary action.

While not all college professors or administrators engage in such behavior, this growing trend is troubling and does not bode well for free speech.

College campuses are not the only place where free speech has become an endangered species. Rather than honestly debate the merits and demerits of an issue, the left now regularly resorts to grotesque name-calling in an attempt to silence the other side. When faced with an honest difference of opinion on policy issues, it has become a favorite tool of the left to call those with whom they disagree Nazis, Klansmen, murders, racists, etcetera.

For example, when Al Gore addressed the National Association for the Advance of Colored People (NAACP) annual convention, rather than defending the merits of affirmative action or race-based preferences, he attacked those who disagree with him, saying, "I've heard the critics of affirmative action. I've heard those who say we have a color-blind society. They use their color blind the way *duck hunters use a duck blind—they hide behind it and hope the ducks won't notice.*"

Hunters use a duck blind to hunt and kill ducks. Is Al Gore implying that affirmative action's critics want to hunt blacks? Precisely. Only a few sentences later in the speech, Gore demanded to know the reaction of his foes to the shocking, racially-motivated dragging death of a black man in Jasper, Texas implying that they approved of such violence.

Such talk was not out of character for Gore. He has made a career of demonizing the opposition. When new water regulations were being debated, Gore's response was to dismiss the opposition as rogue monsters that wanted children to die from drinking dirty, polluted water. For the record, no one was lobbying for dirty water. But, Al Gore was not interested in an honest debate. Vilification and defamation would suffice.

Filmmaker Spike Lee said he would like to "shoot [Charleton Heston] with a .44-caliber Bulldog" revolver. What drew Lee's wrath? He doesn't like Heston's stand on gun control. Most responsible people would challenge Heston to a debate or at least disagree with him on substantive grounds. But Spike Lee, looking at the world through his liberal lens, wants to kill the man.

Perhaps even more interesting is no one in the mainstream media seems bothered by this sort of name-calling and calls for violence. They seem to accept it as within an acceptable norm. In fact, many within the media are among the most irresponsible.

Newsweek writer and political commentator, Eleanor Clift, had this to say about the House managers during the Clinton impeachment, "That herd of managers from the House, I mean, frankly all they were missing was white sheets. They're like night riders…" To state that the House managers were simply murderous Klansmen minus the white sheets is vicious and groundless character assassination that demeans what should have been a serious debate.

Karen Grigsby Bates wrote in the *Los Angeles Times*, "Whenever I hear Trent Lott speak, I immediately think of nooses decorating trees. Big trees, with black bodies swinging…" This is an outrageously false and savage personal attack masquerading as meaningful political debate.

Representative Major Owens (D-NY) publicly stated that congressional Republicans who oppose a minimum wage hike are comparable to foreign despots who engage in "ethnic cleansing"—mass murder. To liberals, this evidently passes as serious comment and insightful debate. To the rest of the word, it is beneath contempt.

In the *Los Angeles Times*, Cartoonist Paul Conrad drew a sketch of Buford Furrow, the murderer and bigot who tried to kill a group of Jewish children at a Jewish community center in Los Angeles and shot and killed a Filipino mailman.

Mr. Conrad labeled his cartoon: "A faith-based compassionate conservative." In other words, religious conservatives are precisely the type of people you'd expect to kill Jewish school children. There is no evidence that this murderer is religious or conservative. Even if he were, it would be well beyond outrageous to tar other religious conservatives as supportive of this murderer's actions and motives.

Whether it's college campuses, political leaders or the media, it appears that the trend for the left has been to spew the most depraved comparisons when talking about conservatives—Hitler, Nazi, racist, the Ku Klux Klan, murderer, etcetera. To many on the left, conservatives are not merely wrong, they're evil and dangerous and must be stopped. Thus, slander, defamation, threats and attempts to silence are all fair game because the ends justify the means.

Because we are blessed to have free speech, those who are fearful of real debate, or not smart enough to engage in it, can continue to viciously attack and defame in hopes of silencing the opposition. However, I am one American who believes that the "market place of ideas" should be invigorated and the debate elevated. That means that politicians must admit that not everyone who disagrees with them is a Nazi, Klansman or murderer. The press must recommit itself to accuracy, fairness and objectivity. And college professors and administrators must become recommitted to academic freedom and free speech—even for conservative students and opinions.

Cracking Down on Fraud and Dishonesty

(Originally published in August 2002)

Recent news has been full of reports of corporate accounting scandals—Enron, Global Crossing, WorldCom and Arthur Anderson to name a few. Through all of this, we learned that some corporations have employed "inventive accounting" to purposefully and fraudulently overstate their income and financial strength. The results were that investors were cheated, confidence in the economy was diminished and companies were bankrupted.

In reaction to such news, Congress quickly passed, and the president signed, legislation designed to crack down on such fraudulent and inaccurate accounting practices. Fortunately, most business leaders are honest. However, those few who have not been honest have imposed significant costs on the rest of us. But, this new law won't make people honest. Perhaps it will discourage overt dishonesty—only time will tell.

Unfortunately, the new law will almost certainly be a green light to greedy lawyers to file more frivolous class-action lawsuits. Whenever a company's stock prices go down or whenever financial data are updated, there will be a flood of litigation. It won't matter that no fraud or "creative accounting" is involved. The threat of the lawsuit alone will provide ample incentive to pay the lawyer bandits their ransom. You and I will ultimately pay for all these lawsuits in higher prices.

One can never go wrong by overestimating the greed and avarice of some attorneys. Thanks to attorneys, we have seen lawsuits by people who spill coffee on themselves and then sue the restaurant complaining that the coffee was hot. We now see lawsuits by overweight people suing fast food restaurants because the burgers and fries are tasty and high in calories. While Congress is cleaning up corporate accounting, perhaps they can clean up the legal business as well. But that is another topic.

Back to the new corporate accounting legislation. No reasonable person will suggest that it is acceptable for corporations or CEOs to fraudulently overstate their profits, cheat and defraud investors or misrepresent the facts in an attempt to artificially maximize their financial position. Such behavior does great harm to the economy and to individuals—stealing life savings for retirement, children's college education or a home.

Let's hope the era of lies and deception is now over. This unfortunate era began in the early years of the last decade. Beginning in the early 1990s, we were told by many in the press and media and in Congress that character did not count, only results mattered. These same folks spent the last decade making excuses for lies, deceptions and ethical shortcuts. They asserted that as long as the stock market and economy were strong, lies and deceptions were no big deal. Most of the media and one-half of the U.S. Senate accepted, embraced and ultimately defended perjury and then congratulated themselves for being broad-minded. Now these same folks are appalled by stories of corporate dishonesty. Perhaps they should look inward.

Today, we know better than to believe that character does not count. Experience tells us that dishonesty has real costs. It harms real people. It can even weaken the economy and the stock market. Strange how a decade ago, honesty did not matter as long as the economy was strong and today we see that dishonesty can weaken both the economy and the stock market. Dishonesty is not quite so clever, acceptable or engaging now.

It is bizarre to hear certain members of Congress lecturing the corporate world that it must be completely honest in its communications and financial dealings. We are now treated to the spectacle of Senator Robert Torricelli (D-NJ), who was recently reprimanded for accepting gifts or what some would call bribes, preaching to corporate America that honesty is the best policy. Senator Tom Daschle (D-SD) ardently defended Torricelli's influence peddling all in the name of election-year politics and maintaining his own political power the same day he preached the necessity of corporate integrity. And many in the mainstream press just mindlessly nod their heads in agreement.

I want corporate America to be honest, but I find it amusing to hear the mainstream media and certain members of Congress delivering the sermon. It is akin to watching Bill Clinton lecture on the importance of marital fidelity. No one would argue with the message, but there has got to be a more credible messenger.

In addition to corporate integrity, we need more honesty in the media and in government. Big government and the big media are among the most corrupt industries in America. The media is amazingly biased, yet it disingenuously maintains its neutrality. Its trust is at all-time lows and still falling, yet they refuse to clean house. Many of those in positions of political power regularly lie and deceive to maintain their position and privilege. This is all done at the expense of the citizenry—the shareholders of this great nation. Perhaps it is time to demand that the media and Congress apply the new corporate honesty laws to themselves.

Daschle's and Gore's Vivid Imaginations

(Originally published in November 2002)

Al Gore made news by picking up on Tom Daschle's theme that Democrats are victims of a right-wing media conspiracy. Daschle's post election rantings were loopy. But Gore, not to be outdone, said that right-wing media sources ultimately control the content of the *New York Times, Washington Post* and CBS News. What planet do these folks live on?

After a disastrous midterm election for his party, Daschle complained that talk radio hosts were responsible because they "attack those…in public life." He went even further to argue that because of talk radio, "people aren't satisfied to just listen…And so…the threats…go up dramatically…" This is utter foolishness.

First, Democrats did not lose the elections because of talk radio. They lost it because they spent the year being obstructionists and posturing for partisan political gain. Voters punished them on Election Day.

Second, Daschle blamed talk radio and Rush Limbaugh for unnamed, uncorroborated and nonexistent "threats." Yet, I have never heard any conservative radio personality incite or encourage violence or intimidation of any sort.

Third, this is not the first time that liberals have attempted to blame conservatives and talk radio. Almost immediately after the Oklahoma City Bombing, liberals began blaming that horrific crime on conservatives. Their reasoning was if you believe government should tax less, spend less and be less intrusive, you were inciting people to bomb federal buildings. That is a gargantuan leap and *if* true, would make a terrorist of even George Washington and Thomas Jefferson. Interestingly, it was not just liberal politicians who parroted this tripe. The mainstream media joined in as well.

Later, Al Gore said, "The media is…truthfully speaking, part and parcel of the Republican Party." He further argued that "ultraconservative billionaires" make deals with Republicans and the media and, over time, weave their talking points into even the more liberal media outlets.

Al Gore has a long history of being detached from truth and reality. After all, he claims he "took the initiative in creating the Internet," and told detailed stories about visiting disaster sites he never visited. Gore has even tried to rewrite history explaining away his legal battles in Florida to exclude unfavorable votes and include only the favorable ones. But let's deal with the substance of what Gore alleges rather than his personal credibility.

First, Gore argues that his message isn't getting out to the public because the media is too influenced by conservatives. Didn't Gore win most of the major media endorsements in the 2000 presidential election? Didn't CBS News' Dan Rather embarrassingly gush about how great Bill and Hillary Clinton were? Aren't the *Washington Post* and *New York Times* almost reflexively liberal? Didn't *ABC News'* Peter Jennings identify virtually every GOP senator as conservative or ultraconservative during the impeachment vote, but never mentioned that Senators Kennedy, Kerry or Biden are "ultraliberals?"

Second, polls have consistently shown that the public sees a liberal media bias. Even self-identified Democrats see the liberal bias. The fact that Al Gore can't see what is plainly evident doesn't speak well of his powers of observation.

Third, it is extraordinarily odd to hear Democrats complain of incivility and harsh criticism. Democrats have accused President George W. Bush of trying to kill seniors—depicting him pushing a wheelchair-bound senior citizen off a cliff. They have accused Republicans of wanting to starve school children, force seniors to eat dog food and kill children with air and water pollution. They have even compared conservatives to the murderous, oppressive and terrorist Taliban regime. Frankly, national Democrats have no moral footing to complain of incivility. They, along with willing accomplices in the media, have made name-calling and incivility a blood sport.

2002 was a bad year for Tom Daschle and Al Gore. Daschle lost the Senate majority. Gore learned that most voters think he shouldn't run in 2004. If they keep throwing childish tantrums and saying demonstrably idiotic and foolish things, next year won't be any better.

Liberal Hate Speech Aimed at Children

(Originally published in March 2003)

Suppose that a public school teacher, whose elementary-aged class included several adopted children of same-sex couples, singled-out the adopted children and told the rest of the class that homosexuality is evil and that their parents are immoral. Can there be any doubt that the teacher would be denounced, fired, blacklisted and made virtually unemployable by any public school nationwide? While I am not an adherent to the gay and lesbian agenda, I also have no interest in singling out children and subjecting them to public scorn and ridicule. The fact that one does not approve of a parent's decisions or behavior should not influence one's treatment of the children.

Recently, some public school teachers in Maine, who teach the children of members of a recently deployed National Guard unit, told their classes that the pending war with Iraq and anyone who would fight in that war are "immoral." There were over thirty complaints from parents. Parents reported that their children were upset, confused, hurt and felt singled-out for criticism and ridicule. Some of the children were as young as seven years old.

The reaction in the media has been surprisingly quiet. A few media outlets covered the story, but the rest yawned. Most of the major media have paid little attention to these events. Perhaps, they agreed with the teachers. But one would think everyone would agree that the children should be spared ridicule and scorn.

Why don't we see the same reaction in the media as we would have if the teacher had labeled homosexuality immoral?

The media, government officials and other teachers would have gone ape over a public school teacher labeling homosexuality as immoral—particularly to children of homosexual partners. Yet when teachers tell children that their parents are immoral because they have been called-up to serve in the National Guard, we see only a few media reports. In less than a week, the issue had largely blown over. Why the difference?

Maine Commissioner of Education J. Duke Albanese has simply stated that the teachers "may have been less than sensitive to children of military families." May have been? Less than sensitive? It is clear the offending teachers will not be fired or disciplined in any real way. What are we to learn from this?

First, liberalism is rife with double standards and hypocrisy. For example, on the issue of the First Amendment's freedom of speech, liberals support only liberal speech. Conservative speech is not worthy of protection. If you criticize the morality of America's fighting men and women, that is protected speech. If you question the morality of homosexuality, that is not protected because it is "hate-speech." If you question the patriotism of the Hollywood left, they howl with anger. Yet, telling young children that their parents are immoral because they are in the military, that is protected free speech. Such double standards pose no significant problem for most liberals.

Second, liberals often justify their actions by claiming to support the interests of children. Yet, as a number of teachers and the top educator in Maine have shown, the children are not truly their primary concern. Years ago, I sat on a public school board. If I had a dollar for every time liberals justified promoting their power and influence by saying, "I'm doing this for the children…," I could own my own newspaper or television station. These folks don't particularly care about children—what they care about is their power and influence. If hiding behind children promotes their power and influence, they gladly invoke the cause of children. But when there is a choice between the children's interests and their interests, the children had better get out of their way or they will be trampled.

Third, liberals support military action depending on who calls for it. When Bill Clinton called for military action and bombed Iraq, Hollywood was pretty quiet. Where were Barbra Streisand, George Clooney, Susan Sarandon, Martin Sheen, Matt Damon and Mike Farrell then? Now that George W. Bush calls for military action, Hollywood is going nuts. If Hollywood wants us to take them seriously, they'll have to stop being for or against everything based solely on partisan politics. Otherwise, they reveal that they are nothing more than mindless, partisan hacks.

The common thread is that current liberalism is not based on principle. It is based on expediency, convenience, and the pursuit of power and self-interest. This is why "liberal" and "liberalism" have become dirty words to most of America.

A Desperate Campaign, an Eager Media and Fraudulent Documents

(Originally published in September 2004)

John Kerry's campaign has been in a free fall since proclaiming he was "reporting for duty" at the Democratic Convention. Then came along Dan Rather and CBS News to Kerry's rescue. The story was perfect—it even had "documentation" that young Lt. George W. Bush did not complete his service in the National Guard. There is only one problem for Kerry, Rather and CBS—the story is based on a fraud. The documents are forgeries and their key source is untruthful.

The documents were purportedly written in 1972 and 1973 by one of Bush's commanders, Lt. Col. Jerry Killian, who died in 1984. But forensic document experts say that the memos are so obviously forgeries that it is surprising CBS ran the story.

William Flynn, a nationally renowned forensic document expert, said, "These sure look like forgeries...these documents could not have existed" in the 1970s. Flynn concludes that the documents are a "hoax."

Richard Polt, a professor at Xavier University and an expert on typewriters, said, "...they are crude and amazingly foolish forgeries. I'm a Kerry supporter, but I won't let that cloud my objective judgment. I am 99% sure these documents were not produced in the early 1970s."

Gary Killian, the son of Lt. Col. Jerry Killian, said the documents did not come from his family and they are "very dubious" because the signatures were not his father's and the wording was not his father's style. He said his father thought very highly of young Lt. George W. Bush. In fact, unquestionably authentic National Guard documents show that Lt. Col. Killian rated Lt. Bush "an exceptionally fine young officer and pilot."

But beyond all this, there at least six reasons even an untrained eye can tell the documents are forgeries.

First, the forged documents are not monospaced, which was standard for typewriters in the 1970s. Instead, the forgeries are proportionally spaced, which is the standard for current word processors and did not commonly exist in 1973. In monospaced format, all letters, whether wide or thin, are spaced the same. In proportional spacing, thin letters like "i" take less space than wide letters like "M."

Second, if one retypes the forged documents using Microsoft Word with the default settings, a perfect copy is produced. The spacing, the font, the line height, even the line breaks are all exactly the same as on the forged documents.

Third, the forgeries use a font called Times New Roman, which was not available to the public in 1973. But the font is the current default setting in Microsoft Word.

Fourth, a 1970s typewriter could not produce the apostrophes in the forgeries. Apostrophes produced by 1970s typewriters were straight vertical marks with no curlicues. The apostrophes in the forged documents were perfect copies of those produced by current word processors.

Fifth, the forged documents used small superscripts to describe the 111th Fighter Squadron. The "th" after the number in the forged memo is much smaller than the other text. However, 1970s typewriters did not have small superscripts. Instead, they produced the "th" in the same size as surrounding text (i.e. 111th Fighter Squadron, not 111th)

Sixth, one of the forged memos named a Col. Walter "Buck" Staudt as pressuring others to "sugar coat" the record. However, Col. Staudt retired and was honorably discharged eighteen months before the date on the forged memo.

Notwithstanding all these warning signs, Dan Rather was so excited to have the "gotcha" story of the year blasting Bush that he failed to notice what average Joes on the Internet could plainly see—the basis of his story was a fraud.

To make matters worse, Rather's star witness, Ben Barnes, who claimed he pulled strings to get young George W. Bush into the National Guard, turns out to have no credibility. Only a few years ago, he said he never helped Bush enter the National Guard. Today, as a key fundraiser for John Kerry, he says otherwise. Barnes' own daughter laments her father's story as false, politically motivated and an opportunistic way to sell his upcoming book.

Now the only questions to be answered are who forged the documents and who gave them to the willing and useful dupe, Dan Rather. It now appears there are close ties to Kerry's campaign.

Pat Caddell, a long time Democratic strategist, opined that if the documents are proved to be forgeries the presidential race "is over"—repeating twice, "It would be the end of the race." Others have suggested that Dan Rather may have ensured the reelection of George Bush. Wouldn't that be a surprise?

A Microcosm of the Media Elite and Bias

(Originally published in September 2004)

The press and media are pulling for John Kerry and John Edwards. This is so obviously true it is almost mundane—like calling a press conference to proclaim the sun rises in the East. But the press and media vociferously deny any bias and become indignant at the mere suggestion of partiality.

Don't take my word for it. The Assistant Managing Editor of Newsweek, Evan Thomas, recently said, "Let's talk a little media bias here. The media, I think, wants Kerry to win. And I think they're going to portray Kerry and Edwards...as being young and dynamic and optimistic and all, there's going to be this glow about them...that's going to be worth maybe 15 points."

The recent scandal involving Dan Rather, CBS News and forged documents is powerful evidence of the mainstream media's intense bias. The forged documents so completely reinforced their own views and prejudices that they overlooked the obvious fact that the documents were sloppy forgeries and their "unimpeachable" sources were laughably unreliable.

The documents upon which Dan Rather built his sensational story questioning the National Guard service of President George W. Bush turned out to be slipshod forgeries produced using a current version of Microsoft Word running on a personal computer, not a 1970s typewriter. To make matters worse, the forgeries refer to an officer in the present tense who had retired 18 months before the date on the memo. Countless experts state that the documents are almost certainly forgeries—including former FBI examiners with more than thirty years' experience. Even CBS's experts are now saying they can't authenticate the documents.

Notwithstanding the overwhelming evidence, Dan Rather and CBS News "stand by" their story—stubbornly maintaining that the forgeries are authentic and the story about Bush is not biased. They even refuse to further investigate the documents or divulge how they got them.

Why won't CBS investigate the authenticity of the documents? The answer is actually quite simple—it would eventually require them to admit wrongdoing. An admission of wrongdoing would end the debate about their bias and destroy their credibility. By ridiculously maintaining that the documents are authentic, they can pretend there is a serious debate on this question and avoid admitting their bias and wrongdoing—at least for a while.

Refusing to acknowledge what is obvious and established is exactly what Alger Hiss did. Hiss was a high-ranking official in the State Department of the Franklin Roosevelt Administration. He was also a communist spy. The evidence was overwhelming and interestingly enough also involved a typewriter. Yet, Hiss denied to his death that he was a spy. Because of his denials, even decades later, loopy apologists continue defending Hiss—despite KGB papers that list the information he stole, his contacts and what he was paid by the communists. Had Hiss admitted the obvious, no one would defend him. But because Hiss refused to admit his crimes, to this very day, he has committed apologists who pretend the matter is still a serious debate.

Rather is following the Hiss strategy of denying what is plainly obvious so as to leave the debate at least partly open. He may at some point apologize for having been misled or making some innocuous error. But Rather will never apologize for lying to America. He will never apologize to America for telling us the documents had been authenticated by experts when they had not been. He will never apologize for standing by his story when everyone knew it was false. He will never apologize for telling us his anonymous sources were "unimpeachable" when they were, in fact, laughable and incredible. This is the Hiss strategy in action. Rather knows that as long as he doesn't admit his wrongdoing, there will be dupes who will defend him and pretend that there is an open debate on these questions.

Perhaps the most interesting question is why Rather and CBS won't divulge all the details of how it came upon these forged documents. What is the point of protecting a "source" that has lied and committed fraud and made you look like a fool? The answer lies in who was involved in the forgeries coming to CBS. The best evidence is that Kerry campaign operatives collaborated with CBS in the matter of the forged documents. We now know that CBS spoke with Joe Lockhart, a top Kerry campaign strategist, and arranged for him to speak with Rather's sources. That not only breaches journalistic standards for ethics, it links John Kerry's campaign to the forged document scandal.

If John Kerry's campaign had absolutely nothing to do with the document scandal story, CBS would gladly be more forthcoming with facts. However, given the media's support for Kerry, Rather cannot now identify the Kerry campaign as one of the perpetrators of this shoddy fraud. To do so would destroy Kerry's election chances. Thus, Rather and CBS steadfastly maintain their reporting was accurate and refuse to divulge all the facts and circumstances surrounding the forgery caper. They simply hope the issue will go away as soon as possible. Perhaps the issue will fade, but the stench around CBS, Rather and the Kerry campaign will not dissipate any time soon.

Another Bush Letter: Maybe Dan Rather is Right

(Originally published in September 2004)

Dan Rather and CBS News have been roundly criticized for using forged documents as the foundation for a "gotcha" story blasting President George W. Bush's service in the National Guard some thirty years ago. The facts were pretty bad for Dan & Co. Even their experts denied authenticating the documents and said that Rather was warned about serious questions before he ran the story and conveniently failed to mention the experts' concerns. The news wasn't any better for John Kerry. It turns out that one of his top campaign strategists was involved in several communications between CBS and the "sources" for the fraudulent story.

But rumor has it that Dan Rather has released one last letter from his collection that may require us all to rethink our criticism. Perhaps we owe an apology to Dan and CBS. You decide. Here is the text of the recently released 1973 letter from George W. Bush to his parents.

"January 12, 1973

"Dear Mom and Dad,

"With my plans to head off to Harvard to earn my MBA, I should tell you that I've had a great time in the National Guard flying fighter jets. I feel fortunate that I could get into the Guard. Thanks, Dad, for exerting your powerful influence to get me in the Guard. I guess when your dad is a future president, you get special privileges. Heck, with me being a future president, maybe I didn't need Dad's powerful influence. Maybe my influence would have been enough.

"They worked us hard in flight training, but we had time for fun too. I bought an Apple iPod MP3 Player. I can download music on the Internet (DSL is way better than dial-up) and hook up the iPod to my wireless network. The iPod is way cooler than my Bose Wave radio or my old Sony Walkman.

"I'm sorry I haven't sent you any pictures lately. Now that I'm in rural Alabama, my cell phone doesn't get a good enough reception for me to send you all the pictures I've taken with the very cool digital camera that's built in.

"I spoke with Lt. Col. Killian and he told me that he had written several unflattering memos about me. But given that Dad and I will one day be presidents, he said he had cut me some slack. He very cleverly made the memos look like forgeries so that when Dan Rather, CBS News and John Kerry attack my Guard service during my second presidential campaign 32 years from now, I will be able to deflect the heat.

"He said he used fonts, spacing formats, superscripts and other typographical elements that have not yet been invented. He also said he asked his wife (who sadly will become a widow in 1984 due to his untimely death) and his son to deny that the memos were written by him so that I would have more credibility. I told Lt. Col. Killian that I was very appreciative for his help. He said it was no problem—he does this sort of thing all the time for people who will be president in 30 years.

"I've got to run to meet some friends at Starbucks. Then we'll grab dinner at the new ESPN Sports Zone. I'll let you know how the food is.

"Love,

"George

"P.S. Make sure you destroy this letter because if John Kerry or Dan Rather get a hold of it, they will learn of Lt. Col. Killian's very tricky plan to help my 2004 presidential campaign."

Let's be serious for a moment. I admit that I fabricated the previous letter. But I haven't been on the news for a week promising America it is genuine. Dan Rather and CBS News are now a laughingstock for their absurd claim that their documents are genuine and their sources "unimpeachable" despite all the evidence against them. This is precisely as it should be. Their "smoking gun" turned out to be a fraud. If Dan Rather's documents are genuine, so is the previous letter from young Lt. George W. Bush to his parents. You be the judge.

The Suicide of Dan Rather, CBS News and Journalism

(Originally published in September 2004)

Dan Rather and the folks at CBS News must be completely mad. There is no credible expert who says Dan's forged documents are authentic. Scores of renowned experts have said they are forgeries. Yet, Dan and CBS stand by their story and now they are demanding that President George W. Bush answer the questions raised in their forged documents. Not satisfied with the lunacy of that demand, Dan Rather goes on to argue that because Bush has not answered to Dan's satisfaction the questions raised in the forged documents, Bush is essentially admitting the charges are true.

Since Dan believes it is legitimate journalism to require folks to answer questions raised in forged and fraudulent documents and since not answering the questions is evidence of the charge's truth, I have some questions for Dan Rather.

I have in my possession a number of admittedly false and forged documents. Each of these documents raises serious questions about Dan Rather. I will list them below and demand that Dan Rather respond to them. If he does not fully answer each of the questions to my satisfaction, it is evidence that the charges implied in the questions are true.

I have an internal CBS document that says Dan Rather detests President Bush and on a daily basis, Rather sets aside his journalistic standards and ethics and misuses his position in the media to misrepresent facts and twist news to make Bush look bad. The documents further state that Dan Rather is as biased as Saddam was cruel and that he also requires CBS employees to slant the news.

Dan Rather must respond to these charges. He cannot simply state that my documents are forgeries. If he does not respond satisfactorily to the substance of the charges, he is admitting they are true.

Another document in my possession states that Dan Rather uses his position and power within CBS News to squash other employees who don't agree with him and won't slant the news. It says disagreeing with Dan Rather is like betraying a mafia don. It also says that Dan uses his power and influence to obtain special treatment and favors.

These are serious issues and Dan Rather must respond. Quibbling about the authenticity of my sources is a diversionary tactic. Refusing to answer the charges is admitting they are true.

I have other documents that suggest Dan Rather was involved in Jimmy Hoffa's disappearance and that he is a Russian spy. I even have a document that says Dan was involved in Abraham Lincoln's assassination.

I realize that Dan may be tempted to dismiss the charges by simply questioning my sources and saying the documents are forgeries, but as Dan Rather has said, "Answer the questions." Refusing to answer only proves the charges true. As Dan said, "The longer we go without a denial of such things—this story is true."

For the record, I am playing the journalism game by Dan Rather's rules. But, I am being a great deal more honest, ethical and fair than Dan Rather because I have openly disclosed my source documents are forgeries. I've made no false claims of authenticity. Tomorrow I will not disingenuously "stand by the story." I will simply ask Dan Rather to "answer the questions" and point out that by Dan's own mouth failure to answer only proves the "story is true."

If this sounds like the Salem witch trials, then you have a much stronger sense of basic fairness, honesty and decency than Dan Rather or CBS News. Dan Rather was once a respected journalist. Today, he is a witless partisan hack and a bad one at that. CBS was once the most respected news organization in America. Today, it is nothing more than a mediocre entertainment company.

Those who ran the Salem witch trials once had power, prestige and the appearance of respectability. However, once their lies, distortions and perverse standards for "fairness" were revealed, they were loathed and dismissed as pathetic figures in history. Such could be the fate of Dan Rather and CBS News.

6

Constitutional Government

The Death of Democracy: Governance by Litigation—a Stealth Assault on America

(Originally published in October 2003)

America's constitutional representative democracy is under attack. This plot is not being carried out by terrorists or an opposing army, but by greedy and power-hungry trial lawyers who seek to overthrow our constitutional representative democracy and install in its place a system of governance by litigation in which lawyers rule supreme. With the assistance and backing of trial lawyers, small and extreme groups are finding it increasingly easy to bypass and subvert the democratic process and impose their agenda on the rest of society by abusing litigation and manipulating the courts.

For example, for years, a small number of political extremists have proposed everything from banning fatty foods to imposing heavy taxes on unhealthy foods. According to these proposals, green beans and carrots would have received a favored tax treatment, but bacon, hamburgers and french fries would all have a very high tax placed on them. These proposals went nowhere in the halls of Congress and in the state legislatures. Why? Because these anti-fat proposals are nutty and the public knows it. Legislators stupid enough to vote for such foolishness would likely lose reelection in all but the most extreme districts. But in a lawsuit, these absurd ideas can take wings and get off the ground—all it takes is one greedy trial lawyer and one judge who is either stupid or has a political agenda to push. The protections afforded by representative democracy are effectively repealed.

One of the turning points for this troubling development of lawyer-run governance came in 1998, when state governments obtained a $246 billion settlement from the tobacco industry. To gain an advantage in the litigation and force the tobacco industry to settle, state governments changed centuries of legal precedent and dramatically loosened age-old checks on the abuse of power. The federal government, seeing the huge sums of money to be obtained, filed a copycat case against the tobacco industry, contravening its own laws in the process and contradicting its earlier public statements that the federal government had no case under the law or the facts.

Some are willing to overlook the lawlessness of the tobacco litigation because it had the effect of punishing the unpopular tobacco companies. However, our justice system is supposed to work for everyone, not just the popular. One of the most sacred things in our constitutional representative democracy is the defense of the unpopular citizen. Popular folks generally do not need constitutional protections—their popularity is their protection. The whole point of the Bill of Rights was to protect the unpopular citizen from an overreaching government. Today, there is a long list of companies and industries that are deemed as not worthy of fair treatment. But this is a dangerous attitude and a perilous precedent. What and who are popular and unpopular changes. You could be next.

We are a nation that claims to follow the rule of law. In a representative democracy, the people are king. The people elect representatives who make the laws and executives (presidents and governors) who carry out the laws. The courts are not elected and do not represent the will of the people. On the federal level, judges have a life term. Thus, the courts are not given the authority to make law. The courts simply adjudicate disputes under the law and faithfully interpret the law.

But in recent years, trial lawyers with the assistance of opinion leaders and some rogue judges, are making, enforcing and adjudicating law without ordinary citizens ever having a chance to address the issues at the ballot box. As a result, legislative proposals that had no real support in the halls of our democratically elected legislatures, eventually find there way into the law thanks to the relentless efforts of trial lawyers who abuse litigation and our court system to achieve their political and financial aims.

For trial lawyers of this ilk, its all about money. They simply do not care what costs they impose on regular folks or on our society.

Stacking the Deck Against Due Process

For years, smokers tried to sue cigarette manufacturers to pay for their medical bills. But they never got away with it—and for good reason. People choose to smoke and they know the risks. Just like people choose to eat too much and know the risks. In a free society, we have the right to make a host of choices. But we must be responsible for our choices.

But this common sense came to an end in 1998. Several states made deals with trial lawyers, throwing out legal precedent and applying new laws retroactively in order to ensure a win against the tobacco companies. The smell of billions of dollars in new revenue was too much to resist for many state governments.

Maryland legislators, for example, rewrote the law after the state filed a lawsuit against the tobacco companies. The changes in the law were designed to guarantee Maryland victory and force tobacco companies to pay the state billions of dollars in an out-of-court settlement rather than risk losing in court. The trial lawyer Maryland hired to handle its lawsuit, Peter Angelos, was so convinced the changed law would guarantee him victory that he promised to cut his legal fee in half—down from $1.1 billion to $500 million—if the state would change the law to favor him and the lawsuit. The state obliged. The tobacco companies realized they had no chance at a fair trial, so they settled and paid the state billions of dollars. All went as planned, except that Angelos demanded the full legal fee of $1.1 billion anyhow.

It's all about the money. The law can be a casualty, constitutional principles can be discarded and fairness can be cast aside as long as they get their money.

Checks on our legal system are under attack and are steadily eroding, making it possible to win cases that defy rationality. This is why we hear about obese people suing fast food restaurants for providing tasty super-sized french fries. Sure its nuts. But, if just one judge will see things their way, they get a huge payday. And just because a lawsuit takes place in one state does not mean the verdict is limited to that state. A case in a single courtroom, in a single jurisdiction, with a single judge, is all it takes to force an industry to pay billions in out-of-court settlements and change its business practices everywhere in the United States. Shouldn't these sorts of major public policy decisions be made by our democratically elected representatives?

Yet in recent years, many of these decisions have effectively been made by trial lawyers whose influence in the political system has grown to such an extent that age-old legal institutions, which had acted as a restraint on their objectives, have begun to break down. The more cases trial lawyers win, the wealthier and more politically active they become, enabling them to ram through even more lawyer-friendly legislation. Among those changes, it has become easier to "forum shop," allowing lawyers to shop around for judges or jurisdictions sympathetic to their agendas. It is also easier to allow testimony from hired "experts" brought in to support those agendas, even if those witnesses are well outside the accepted standards of their field. Moreover, the rise of class action lawsuits enable lawyers to sue with no real clients. And now "negligence" means failing to prevent any conceivable bodily harm—regardless of how many precautions were taken or what responsibility the plaintiff may actually bear.

In 1994, the State of Florida went so far as to change the law to prohibit defendants from presenting certain evidence and legal arguments, making it all but impossible to defend themselves. For the tobacco case, Florida required that defendants post a bond of 150% of the lower court judgment before they could appeal. The bond amount was so cost prohibitive that the right to an appeal was effectively denied.

Stealth Taxation

Much of this out-of-control litigation problem is fueled by the states' voracious appetites for more and more of our money. Americans are already taxed to the hilt, so new taxes are not popular. Thus when politicians go on pork spending sprees, they are often afraid to raise taxes any higher to pay for their excesses. Therefore, free-spending state governments are opting for an alternative revenue source—shaking down deep-pocketed industries through litigation.

Taxation through litigation is now a favorite way for states to cover large budget deficits. For example, it is no coincidence that the states that persist in suing Microsoft all have large projected budget deficits. Despite the fact that the vast majority of states either settled their claims along with the federal government or opted not to get involved in the first place, a few states spend taxpayer money pursuing continued litigation in hopes of a big payday. It's all about money.

This sort of thing is much easier to do when you can demonize an industry and convince the public that the company or industry being attacked is evil. The purpose of the demonization strategy is two-fold: first, to turn public opinion against the company or industry so that the public will tolerate the abusive legal tactics used in the shakedown, and second, to give the appearance that those doing the shakedown are not common thugs or thieves, but are serving the public interest and doing some greater societal good. Instrumental in this demonization strategy is an alliance of extreme activists groups, the media, trial lawyers and government officials, all working to whip up public scorn against certain industries or companies. With strong political and public opinion winds against them, these industries hardly have a chance in the courtroom, regardless of how solid their legal positions are.

An equally troubling development is that federal government has gotten in on the game. After realizing it lost out on getting any of the states' tobacco settlement money, the Clinton Justice Department sued the industry on its own. In doing so, it ignored the law and its own previous congressional testimony. In 1997, the Justice Department testified before Congress that the law did not permit it to sue the tobacco industry to pay for Medicare expenses. But in 1999 the Justice Department filed a case anyway in hopes of a big settlement and another big payday. It's all about money.

Among the federal government's trumped-up charges against tobacco companies was "racketeering"—a law passed to stop organized crime. What had the tobacco companies done that resembled the mob? They sent out press releases in which they questioned government data on health risks and addictions. In the administration's eyes, questioning their data constituted "mail fraud," punishable under racketeering laws meant for the mob. A similar posting on a company website was deemed "wire fraud." In essence, the Clinton administration's definition of racketeering and organized crime was simply making statements with which the administration disagreed.

It is increasingly easy to apply laws arbitrarily—to use the law to selectively target one group or individual for financial or political reasons. This is a phenomenon commonplace in many third-world countries and dictatorships. Such corruption should not exist in America.

Everyone is a Potential Target

The successful lawsuit against the tobacco industry proved that it is possible to cripple any industry by litigation. Trial lawyers' jobs are easier, of course, when that industry manufactures a product disliked by many Americans. But an industry does not even have to be widely hated to be sued. Latex glove makers are not disliked by the American public. Yet, one state attorney general says he wants to bring to bear the whole litigation process on the latex glove industry. Another target is manufacturers of lead-based paint, even though lead paint has not been manufactured in over fifty years and was voluntarily discontinued as soon as it was known that it could be harmful when not properly maintained.

Others ripe for getting sued include makers of candy, fast food, high fat foods, dairy products and beef, since, like tobacco, they all "contribute to federal health care expenditures." A Yale professor claims "there is no difference between Ronald McDonald and Joe Camel." The Physicians Committee for Responsible Medicine is calling for a class-action suit against the meat industry, claiming "meat consumption is just as dangerous to public health as tobacco use."

Breweries and wineries are potential targets as well. They could be forced to pay for medical treatment and other damages to people injured or killed by drunk drivers. Personal responsibility no longer matters that much. Carmakers are vulnerable, too. Some argue that sports cars and cars with powerful engines are defective by design because drivers are tempted to drive dangerously. Thus, they argue that carmakers should pay the costs of damages caused by recklessly driven automobiles. Again, the responsibility and choices of the driver are ignored. It's all about the shakedown and the money.

A society that allows smokers who know what they are doing to shift the blame to others will also eventually allow overweight people to sue fast food restaurants for offering super-sized fries. This is why precedent matters.

Billions of Dollars in Blood Money

The harm being inflicted on our democratic institutions is troubling enough. But there is another sinister element in all of this—extortion. In the underworld, bad guys threaten people, forcing them to hand over their money or suffer the consequences. But why be a mobster when you can go to law school and do the same thing legally? Simply notify a large company that you are suing them, talk them down to the investment world so their stock prices drop and promise the company that if they settle and pay you large sums, you will leave them alone and even talk their stock back up in the investment world. This sort of work pays well, very well. And that is what's important—the money.

A new class of multimillionaires has come into existence. Traditionally, people get rich by creating something of value and selling it. Now, we have a class of people who get rich by producing nothing—they simply extort. It is legalized theft. Apart from the questionable ethics involved, it is simply bad for the economy and every single American pays the price. Every dollar that companies or individuals have to forfeit to greedy lawyers means one less dollar for productive investment, one less dollar to pay hardworking wage earners, one less dollar for job creation.

Moreover, the poor and middle class are often stuck with the bill. Who is ultimately paying for the $246 billion tobacco settlement over the next twenty-five years? It is the 25% of Americans who smoke. More than half of them make under $30,000 a year.

Meanwhile, lawyers are using their newfound wealth to fuel the vicious circle, contributing heavily to like-minded judges, state attorneys general, members of Congress and others, who enact even more lawyer-friendly laws and stifle any attempt at reform.

Freedom in Danger

Some folks simply do not care what happens to big corporations like the tobacco companies, automakers, chemical and drug companies, gun manufacturers and fast food chains. But it is the broader picture that is important here. Unless we stop this cancer in its tracks now, similar things will happen to other businesses, individuals and groups. We are slowly surrendering our constitutional representative democracy to a system of lawyer-run governance.

Our forefathers pledged their lives, fortunes and sacred honor to obtain freedom and throw off the shackles and unjust burdens of an unelected, life-tenured king. Did General Washington's army make those sacrifices and win a glorious victory only to have trial lawyers and unelected, life-tenured judges take the king's place, sack the rule of law and turn our representative democracy into governance by litigation?

We must preserve our constitutional heritage and right to representative democracy. To do less than this would be to stand idly by and watch the end of the greatest revolution in freedom that the world has ever known.

The Cornerstone of America's Freedom

(Originally published in September 2002)

America's famed Constitution was adopted on September 17, 1787. That is long enough ago that most of us take for granted the rights protected by this governing document. But if given a chance to reflect, what constitutionally protected rights do Americans think are the most fundamental to our freedom? I conducted an informal poll, asking this question. The answer came almost universally—free speech and free press. These are reasonable answers. Both of these liberties form a part of the bedrock foundation upon which our freedom is based. But they are not the cornerstone of our freedom.

So what is the cornerstone of the freedom that America has enjoyed for more than 215 years? Oddly enough, the cornerstone to the freedom we enjoy is found in our rights to property—our economic rights. The right to own and control one's property and the fruits of one's labor is the cornerstone of our freedom. Why? How can the right to own something be more important than free speech and press? The answer is simple. Without property rights, no other important right can long survive. Property rights are the soil in which all other rights can grow and thrive.

In the totalitarian regime of the former Soviet Union, for example, communist dictators did not need to outlaw free speech and press to control the populace. All they really needed to do was revoke all property rights. Without property rights and economic freedom, the people lack the independence to exercise other rights. When the government controls who gets the jobs and who gets housing and consumer goods, the people become completely dependent upon the government—for food, shelter, transportation, medicine, education and everything else. Even if legally permitted, few citizens would publicly criticize a government that, if it did not appreciate the criticism, had the authority to take their job, their home and everything else they own.

Without the independence and autonomy provided by the right to own and control the fruits of one's labor and one's property, few other rights amount to much. For this reason, property rights are the cornerstone of the freedoms Americans now enjoy. Unfortunately, too many Americans view property rights as something that concerns only ranchers and farmers in the West. The truth is that property rights impact us all. If you pay income taxes, sales taxes, Social Security taxes or property taxes, if you own a home or a car, if you have a savings account or retirement account, or own stock—you have a stake in protecting property rights.

America's property rights are under siege. High taxes take from workers the fruits of their labors. Thomas Jefferson warned against a spendthrift government that unnecessarily took from the "laborer the bread he has earned." Certain environmental regulations prevent landowners from the reasonable use and control of their own homes, farms and ranches. Other regulations burden individuals and businesses and limit their ability to direct their labors and business affairs. Thomas Jefferson warned that if the government directed "us when to sow and when to reap, we should soon want for bread." The attacks on property rights never seem to end. Then, when someone stands up to defend the cornerstone of our freedom, they are too often labeled "greedy" by the very people who lead the assault on property rights.

As America remembers and celebrates the rights we all enjoy and the Constitution that outlines and protects those rights, we would do well to remember the forgotten right—the right that provides the environment of independence in which all other rights can flourish—property rights. It's an American tradition worth saving.

Court Jesters: The Pledge of Allegiance is Unconstitutional

(Originally published in July 2002)

The Pledge of Allegiance is unconstitutional—or so we are told by a federal appellate court located in California. By a 2-to-1 margin, the Ninth Circuit Court of Appeals held that allowing school children to recite the Pledge is an impermissible establishment of religion. One judge had the good sense to dissent from the holding, but the other two simply defied logic, legal reasoning and the Constitution.

To say the court's ruling is outrageous is like saying the sinking of the Titanic was unfortunate or that the events of September 11th were unpleasant. With their ruling, these two judges have effectively turned in their judicial robes and become court jesters.

I appreciate humor as much as the next guy, but this simply is not funny. This ruling provides a clear and vivid example of why all Americans should oppose activist judges who ignore the Constitution, the law, established historical precedent and the will of the people—and instead impose their will on the rest of us by judicial fiat.

Allowing students to recite the Pledge of Allegiance is no more an establishment of religion than allowing students to study the Declaration of Independence which states that "all men are endowed by their Creator with certain unalienable Rights..." and also refers to "God" by name. If allowing students to say the Pledge is unconstitutional, perhaps students will next be barred from buying school lunches with money imprinted with the words, "In God We Trust." These judges apparently believe the Constitution bans use of the word "God."

Their ruling shows a profound misunderstanding of both the Constitution and our history. On the issue of freedom of religion, the Constitution forbids the government (1) to establish a religion, and (2) to prohibit the free exercise of religion. For the record, the words "separation of church and state" do not appear anywhere in the Constitution. The actual words are: "Congress shall make no law respecting an establishment of religion, or prohibiting the free exercise thereof..." Merely uttering the word God is not the establishment of a religion.

Years ago, the U.S. Supreme Court ruled, correctly in my estimation, that the government could not require or force students to recite the Pledge. But these two judges went well beyond prohibiting forced recitation of the Pledge. They ruled that allowing school children to recite the Pledge was unconstitutional and an "establishment of religion." If their absurd ruling stands, school children will be prohibited from beginning their school day reciting the Pledge of Allegiance.

These two judges are so far off base and so wildly out of the mainstream, and have so completely tortured the plain language of the Constitution that they have violated their oath of office to uphold the Constitution. They have no right to impose their wacky views and opinions on the rest of us. To do so is judicial tyranny and does violence to the Constitution itself.

The Ninth Circuit Court of Appeals has a well-deserved reputation for legal lunacy. It is the most liberal and the most frequently overturned federal appeals court in the entire nation. It is now obvious why.

What most folks don't know is that many of the Ninth Circuit's past decisions when on appeal to the U.S. Supreme Court could not win even a single vote of support—not even from the Supreme Court's liberal justices. For example, in 1998, when five cases appealed from the Ninth Circuit to the U.S. Supreme Court, all five cases were overturned on 9-to-0 votes. Not a single justice, not even the liberal ones, could bring themselves to cast a vote for the Ninth Circuit's zany decisions. But now America has even more striking evidence of the insanity of the Ninth Circuit—these brazen judicial activists believe that reciting the Pledge of Alliance is unconstitutional.

This case illustrates the need for solid judges who will faithfully interpret the Constitution and our laws. To this end, President George W. Bush has submitted to the Senate a number of highly qualified nominees for the federal bench—nominees who will interpret the law and Constitution as they are written, rather than imposing their views and opinions. Yet, for more than 412 days, Senators Tom Daschle and Patrick Leahy have obstructed, delayed and refused even to schedule a hearing for the vast majority of President Bush's appellate court nominees. Perhaps the Ninth Circuit is trying to provide a vivid illustration why Daschle, Leahy & Company should stop the obstruction and delay and perform their constitutional duties.

The Pledge and Forest Fires—One Crazy Court

(Originally published in July 2002)

In one week, two seemingly unrelated stories dominated the news: (i) the Pledge of Allegiance was ruled unconstitutional, and (ii) massive forest fires in the West raged out-of-control, burning millions of acres and destroying homes and animal habitat. Yet, as odd as it may seem these headline-grabbing stories are related—the Ninth Circuit Court of Appeals is at the center of both stories.

By now everyone knows about the absurd Pledge decision—that school kids voluntarily reciting the Pledge somehow violates the First Amendment's prohibition against government establishing a religion. But few know that in 1997, the Ninth Circuit also ruled that the U.S. Forest Service could not manage federal forests or take steps to reduce the risk of forest fires. Now, we see the results—forest fires so large, so intense, and so devastating that over a million acres have been destroyed and heroic efforts to contain the fires have not yet been successful.

But the Ninth Circuit oddities don't end there. One of the judges who voted to ban the Pledge—Judge Stephen Reinhardt—also voted to prohibit management of national forests, which led to conditions favorable to out-of-control fires. Moreover, the single dissenting vote in the Pledge case, Ferdinand Fernandez, was also the sole dissenting vote to what should be called the Forest Fire case.

In a single week, we witnessed two vivid examples of what happens when liberal judicial activists ignore the law and impose their will—the Pledge is banned and the forests burn. The zany ruling on the Pledge dominated the headlines. However, the ruling that turned our national forests into tinderboxes in Arizona and throughout the West has been overlooked.

Here are the facts. Forest management is important to forest health. Forests that are not properly managed build up "fuel loads" as undergrowth, brush and dying and dead trees accumulate on the forest floor. After years of fuel accumulation, when a fire starts, it is so well-fed that it burns out-of-control—destroying the forest, animal habitat and property; filling the air with pollution; and endangering life. However, when a forest is properly managed and a fire starts, it is not as well-fed. As a result, the fire is not as intense and it is easier to control and extinguish—saving forest and animal habitat.

In 2000, 7.5 million acres of forest and wildlife habitat were burned in forest fires thanks to the decision to not manage national forests. Selective thinning of forests improves forest health and reduces fuel loads, which reduces the risk of out-of-control forest fires. In fact, while flying over forests in Northern California, one can readily see the difference between federal and private forests. The private forests are healthier and more vibrant in color. Why? Because private forests are managed by owners who want to maintain the value of their property. Federal forests are managed by goofy court decisions.

The fires are another object lesson in the dangers of letting activist courts manage forests. So far in Arizona alone, about 500,000 acres have burned and 32,000 people have evacuated their homes. The loss of animal life and habitat is staggering. Even larger forest fires have been burning in Colorado. These fires could have been minimized by the very forest management programs the Ninth Circuit prohibited.

To be fair, the Ninth Circuit is not the only culprit. Extreme environmentalists have worked for years to stop forest management in the name of protecting species—thereby encouraging fire conditions that kill species and destroy habitat. The extremist's hostility to forest management is so strong that they prefer to stop all timber production—even removal of only fallen or dead trees—rather than manage forests to reduce risks of serious forest fires.

Nonetheless, despite the goals and objectives of extreme environmentalists, it was the Ninth Circuit who gave them victory. Our forests have been suffering ever since.

Both the Pledge case and the Forest Fire case illustrate the harm that is done by activist judges who seek to impose their political will rather than faithfully interpret the law. President George W. Bush understands the harm done by out-of-control and unaccountable activist judges. Thus, he has nominated highly qualified individuals who will faithfully interpret the law and the Constitution. Yet, Senators Tom Daschle and Patrick Leahy have obstructed, delayed and refused even to schedule a hearing for the vast majority of President Bush's appellate court nominees—some who would serve on the Ninth Circuit and bring a measure of sanity to an otherwise harebrained court. Perhaps, the raging forest fires and the Pledge case will awaken Americans to the need for reliable and reasonable judges.

Obstructionism and Feigned Bipartisanship

(Originally published in March 2002)

One year after then-Republican Senator Jim Jeffords of Vermont announced that he would switch parties and throw control of the United States Senate to the Democrats and make Tom Daschle (D-SD) the Senate Majority Leader, Daschle and the Democrats are celebrating the anniversary of their rise to power. However, it will be an empty celebration because Daschle and his allies have done virtually nothing except obstruct, block and oppose the president.

Even the Democrats' much-ballyhooed bipartisanship after the September 11th attacks was mostly imaginary. Daschle and Company feigned bipartisanship because they could not afford to be seen as partisan obstructionists. After the attacks of September 11th, America expected cooperation. Daschle knew this so he gave the appearance of bipartisanship—at least for while. But it did not take long before even the appearance was gone.

A review of the U.S. Senate's "accomplishments" over the past year reveals that Daschle and Company have been shockingly partisan, antagonistic and obstructionist.

Over one year has passed since President Bush nominated eight highly qualified individuals to various federal circuit courts. Recently, one of the eight nominees finally received a hearing. The remaining seven are still waiting. The American Bar Association rated each of the nominees as qualified or well qualified. The previous three presidents had more than 90% of their circuit court nominees confirmed in less than one year. Yet, Tom Daschle and Patrick Leahy (D-Vt.) have not even held a hearing for seven of the nominees.

Daschle and Company blocked the president's plan to help America produce more of its own energy and thereby reduce America's dependence on Middle Eastern oil. Instead, they pushed an energy bill that only Saddam Hussein could love. But now is not the time to empower Saddam because he has oil that we need. Rather than making it possible for America to produce more of its own energy, Daschle and Company blocked drilling on only 2000 acres of frozen tundra in Alaska. One is left to wonder whether they think sending American soldiers to fight and die in the Middle East is preferable to making our nation less dependent on foreign oil.

Daschle and Company have fought President Bush's efforts to defend Americans from missile attacks. Several nations—China and North Korea, for example—have threatened America with missiles. Other rogue nations are developing missile technology. President Bush is simply doing what he promised to do—protect and defend Americans from missile threats. Why do Senators Daschle and Carl Levin (D-Mich.) work behind the scenes to prevent America from defending itself against missile attack?

Daschle and Company have done everything in their power to prevent an economic turnaround so that they can blame the weak economy on President Bush and improve their chances on election day. They want America to suffer economically until November, in hopes that they will benefit. To this end, they have bottled up the president's economic stimulus package and prevented last year's tax cuts from becoming permanent. They want tax increases in a time of economic weakness.

But the icing on the cake is that Daschle and other Democrats accused the president of knowing the details of the September 11th attack before it happened and doing nothing to prevent it. This is absurd, even by Dan Rather's standards. The administration had only general, nonspecific warnings of possible attacks. There was no specific information about when, where or how the attacks might happen. Information revealing that we have enemies that would like to harm us is simply not new or useful. Yet, Democrats outrageously pretended that the president knew all the relevant facts and simply did nothing. They knew better, but it is an election year. They backed off only when polling showed that the public wasn't buying it and was likely to punish Democrats in the midterm election for being demagogues.

One week later, however, Daschle and Company began criticizing the president for making public information about increased threats of additional terrorist attacks. Senator Daschle, you cannot have it both ways—one week charging that the president was irresponsible because he had very general, non-specific information that was not made public and the next week claiming the president is irresponsible because he makes public information about terrorist threats. This is only the tip of the proverbial iceberg. Suffice it to say, Daschle and Company have used every argument they could devise to oppose the president.

So as Tom Daschle celebrates his rise to power one year ago, one is left to ask, why should we celebrate? Are we better off without qualified judges? Are we better off continuing our dependence on foreign oil? Are we better off without a defense against missile attack? Are we better off if the economy struggles until after the November midterm elections? Are we better off if the Senate is used to undermine the president's national security plans? As Tom Daschle celebrates his rise to power and boasts of what he has done *for* America, reasonable Americans review his record and ask, "What has he done *to* America?"

Inmates Now Running the Asylum

(Originally published in March 2002)

After attending the Senate Judiciary Committee hearing on the nomination of Judge Charles Pickering to the United States Court of Appeals for the 5th Circuit, it became clear that the Senator Leahy and his fellow Democrats on the committee had no interest in the facts or Judge Pickering's qualifications. This was a dirty political smear by some of the Senate's most rancorous and partisan members. Like an angry and irrational mob, they came for a lynching. And before the night was done, they got what they came for.

Watching Democrats march in lockstep to kill this nomination sends a chilling signal about the lengths to which Daschle and his troops will go to frustrate the constitutional process of advise and consent. I sat dumbfounded as I listened to Democrat after Democrat read prepared statements filled with outright lies that even they knew to be false and misleading.

They said that Judge Pickering interjected his personal opinions into the cases he decided. Yet, over the course of more than ten years on the bench as a Federal District Court Judge, his decisions have been overturned at a rate of less than one half of 1%. That is substantially better than the national average for federal judges.

They said Judge Pickering lacked the judicial temperament to be a Circuit Court judge, yet the liberal-leaning ABA gave him their highest rating—"well qualified."

A group of all-white senators said that Judge Pickering lacked "racial sensitivity." Yet African American civil rights leaders, attorneys, and former leaders of the National Association for the Advancement of Colored People (NAACP) lined up to support Judge Pickering. In the 1960s, Charles Pickering testified against an Imperial Wizard of the Klu Klux Klan who had bombed and killed a local civil rights leader.

Not to be out done, Senate Majority Leader Tom Daschle told this whopper—he could not honor President Bush's request for a vote of the full Senate on Judge Pickering's nomination because the president was asking the Senate 'to break a 200-year tradition.' What Tom Daschle lacks in honesty and candor, he attempts to make up for in smooth-talking sophistry. Clarence Thomas and Robert Bork both received a vote from the full Senate despite not receiving a majority vote of support from the committee. I don't know what 200-year tradition he is referring to, but it is clear that Daschle is not tethered to the truth.

I could hardly believe my ears when Russ Feingold said he could not support Judge Pickering because he believed that the highest ethical standards must be upheld. This is ridiculous. The ABA, which has been no friend to conservatives, gave its highest rating to Judge Pickering after an exhaustive review of his legal work, ethics and past. But the ABA's highest rating—which many Democrats refer to as the "gold standard"—somehow was not good enough on this day.

Where was Russ Feingold during the Clinton impeachment hearings? I don't recall a single Democratic Senator having the slightest concern for the "highest ethical standards" at that time. All we heard were equivocations and fabrications back then. Are we to assume that all these Democratic Senators now see the light and have learned the importance of ethics?

The bottom line is this—Judge Pickering should have been confirmed. He is highly qualified. He is highly experienced. He meets every reasonable standard that one could devise. It is quite clear that had the full Senate voted on the nomination, Judge Pickering would have been overwhelmingly confirmed. He had strong support on both sides of the aisle.

But he was not confirmed because Tom Daschle, Harry Reid, Patrick Leahy and Ted Kennedy decided to make sure that the full Senate never got a chance to vote on Judge Pickering. So, the Democrats on the Judiciary Committee dutifully voted not to confirm and to prohibit the full Senate from hearing the matter, even though some of them about ten years ago voted with a unanimous Senate to confirm Judge Pickering to the federal bench. Was it Judge Pickering that had changed during those ten years? Or was it the Senate's character that has changed? The Senate under Tom Daschle's control is an ugly place. The Judiciary Committee under Patrick Leahy's control is a dark place.

Please excuse my disgust at what currently passes for statesmanship. I suppose this is what happens when you let small-minded partisans like Tom Daschle, Harry Reid, Ted Kennedy and Patrick Leahy run the U.S. Senate. Unfortunately, the inmates are now running the asylum.

Incumbency Protection, Free Speech Infringement, Corruption and Potato Chips

(Originally published in February 2002)

The U.S. House of Representatives passed legislation it misleadingly calls "campaign finance reform." If truth in labeling laws applied to legislation, this bill would be called, "The Incumbency Protection, Corruption Promotion and Free Speech Infringement Act." We are told that so-called campaign finance reform laws will take the money out of politics, make elections more competitive, and reduce corruption. Nothing could be farther from the truth.

Champions of so-called campaign finance reform purposefully do not disclose that it takes a lot of money to defeat an incumbent politician. Incumbents already have high name identification. They have a large paid staff. Incumbents can send mail for free to voters during most of the year. All of this is paid for by us and is done so that we know who the incumbent is and what a "wonderful" job he has done. A challenger doesn't have any of these perks. He must raise his own money to pay for printing, postage, staff, press secretaries, office space and commercials to let the voters know who he is and what he stands for.

Incumbent politicians support "campaign finance reform" so that they can limit their opponent's ability to raise money and ensure their own perpetual reelection. On top of that, supporting "campaign finance reform" has the added public relations benefit of making it appear that they oppose politics as usual—when, in fact, campaign finance reform is all about maintaining politics as usual. What a racket!

But it gets even worse. Last year, when this debate was raging in Congress, the very folks who claimed they wanted to keep money out of politics included a loophole that says if a member of Congress is running against a millionaire challenger, the limits do not apply to the incumbent. Why? Because a millionaire challenger can self-finance his campaign and wouldn't be hampered by campaign limits. Thus, the millionaire challenger can be competitive even with the strict campaign limits. But, incumbent politicians don't want competitive races. They want easy elections that guarantee their continued power and influence. So, they support "campaign finance reform" to cripple their opponents ability to competitively challenge them. And if their opponent is a millionaire who cannot be financially crippled, they don't want campaign finance rules to apply.

Simply stated, these duplicitous politicians say that large political contributions are corrupting unless their opponent is a millionaire—then big contributions are okay. The cold, hard truth is that "campaign finance reform" is simply incumbency protection and it will only increase corruption by insulating incumbent politicians from voter accountability.

On top of all of that, campaign finance reform violates our First Amendment rights. Let's suppose Congress proposed a law that prohibited anyone from printing more than 1,000 copies of any political pamphlet or determined that the pamphlet could be distributed only during certain times of the year. The bill's sponsors might argue that the First Amendment is not violated because the law would not dictate what the pamphlet could say. The law would only limit how many copies the publisher could print and when they could distribute it.

I hope the protest would be immediate and loud! The freedom to speak your mind isn't worth much if the government can regulate when and how widely you can express yourself. Thus, even if the government did not censor our words, if they limit our ability to communicate our ideas, they have violated our constitutional rights and severely harmed the cause of freedom.

This is precisely what the U.S. House of Representatives did when it voted in favor of "campaign finance reform." Simply stated, the so-called reform would significantly limit the degree to which you can support a candidate or political cause or an issue you find important. Their "reform" would limit the amount you can donate, to whom you can donate, what can be done with the donated funds and when the funds can be spent.

Is it a good idea to have government dictate and regulate how much you can give to a political candidate and to whom, when and how your money can be used? The answer should clear to anyone who appreciates the freedoms for which our forefathers fought and died.

The most common reason given for supporting this bill is that America spends too much money on politics and elections. What does that mean? What is the correct amount to spend? Perhaps others know how much is the "right" amount. But I doubt it. The reason there is so much money spent on congressional elections is because government has become so big and so powerful. If your goal is to get the money out of elections, perhaps you should start by getting the power out of Washington. Let's be honest, people don't donate large sums to local elections for dogcatcher. But they do for Congress. Why? Because the dogcatcher can't tax or regulate them out of existence. But, Congress can and does. So if you want to reform federal elections, perhaps we should get back to smaller, less intrusive government.

One last thought—spending a lot of money to promote an informed citizenry, free elections and representative government is not necessarily a bad thing. America spends more money on potato chips each year than it does on elections. So why don't those who support campaign finance reform stop monkeying with the First Amendment, stop promoting their own reelection, stop promoting a climate in which corruption will flourish and do something productive—like reducing the cost of potato chips?

Political Speech and Pornography

(Originally published in March 2002)

The Shays-Mehan/McCain-Feingold "campaign finance reform" bill that made its way through the House and the Senate and was signed by President George W. Bush is repugnant to a free society. It promotes corruption, it reduces accountability, it protects incumbent politicians from competition and it limits political speech and debate. Under the First Amendment it is the most important of all forms of speech. But unbelievably, when this bill becomes law the day after November's mid-term elections, pornography will receive greater First Amendment protection than political speech.

This so-called reform bill grants government the power to heavily regulate political speech year round and to essentially ban the most effective forms of political speech during the sixty days before an election and the thirty days before a primary. The bill also significantly limits the degree to which Americans can support issues and causes.

Political speech and debate are fundamental to the foundation of a free and democratic society. Such speech is even more critical during the days and weeks before an election. Yet, the Senate is prepared to regulate and effectively outlaw many forms of political speech when it is most needed and useful.

Would the Senate ban pornography ninety days each year? For example, would they ban pornography during the sixty days before Christmas and Hanukkah and thirty days before Easter and Passover? Under our current law and under the Court's interpretation of the Constitution, even pornography is protected under the First Amendment 365 days a year. But so-called campaign finance reform will empower the government to limit and regulate *political* speech year round and even completely ban it ninety days out of the year.

If pornography, which does nothing to enhance democracy, is protected by the First Amendment and therefore not regulated, why should political speech, which is fundamental to our democracy, be given less First Amendment protection from government regulation? If pornography is not banned ninety days each year, why should some political speech be banned ninety days of each year? Is it a good idea to protect pornography while attacking, regulating and in some cases banning legitimate political debate?

It is bizarre, this world in which we live. Who would have guessed that in America pornography is protected by the First Amendment, but political speech is not? I suppose this is what happens given the current leadership in the Senate.

To understand why we have First Amendment protections for speech and press, one need only know what happened in Boston, Philadelphia, Williamsburg and New York in the months and years before July 4, 1776. When American colonists complained about the abuses of the King or Parliament, their homes and businesses were ransacked and burned and their printing presses destroyed. Thus, the Founders included this language in our Bill of Rights: "Congress shall make no law…abridging the freedom of speech, or of the press; or the right of the people peaceably to assemble, and to petition the Government for a redress of grievances."

Yet, unprincipled incumbent politicians who want easy lifetime reelection and who want to wear the "reformer" label—no matter how unwarranted—lined up to support this bill. Some who professed to oppose the bill, even voted for procedural maneuvers that insured the bill's passage. This is two-faced hypocrisy. It is as if they purposefully unlock the door to your home so that vandals may enter, but then stridently assure you that they oppose the vandalism committed by the very people they knowingly allowed to enter.

I realize some who supported this measure did so in good faith and had no ill motives. But that does not change the fact that they were dead wrong to support such an ill-conceived law.

Others said they voted yes because they are confident the courts will overturn it and declare it unconstitutional. Presumably, they wanted to say yes to the popular but unconstitutional bill and have the courts be the ones to say, "no." That is not a particularly courageous stand. Politicians would do well to remember that in the long run good policy is good politics. More importantly, those who voted yes for a bill they knew was unconstitutional violated their oath of office to uphold and preserve the Constitution. This personal duty cannot be shifted to the courts. Plus, given the general disarray of our court system, how can anyone be confident that the courts will get right what they got so wrong?

An American with a Dream

(Originally published in April 2002)

Senator Tom Daschle (D-SD) has enjoyed a great deal of praise and criticism lately. Thanks to his skillful politicking, he has successfully played the spoiler on many occasions. Some praise his obstructionism. Others decry it. But no one can question his effectiveness. Anger and frustration have caused more than one fellow legislator to question his motives, methods and sense of fair play. However, even the most direct attack often ends with "he is an honorable man."

How can this be? How can Daschle criticize our war efforts and a war-time president; stall, gut, kill, twist, and otherwise derail White House efforts to strengthen the economy and our national security—for partisan advantage—and still be seen as an "honorable man?" The answer is not that complicated. Tom Daschle loves America. He wants to make America a better place. He has a dream of what America can and should be. He works tirelessly to achieve that dream. Tom Daschle and his party are marching towards the America he envisions in his dream.

It is Tom Daschle's dream that scares me. It should terrify anyone who believes that our Founding Fathers set this country on the proper path.

Tom Daschle is fighting for an America much different than that envisioned by Thomas Jefferson, John Adams and George Washington. He is doing all he can to steer us toward a country in which all Americans are equally poor and equally oppressed.

In Tom Daschle's America, plants and animals are more important than people. There can be no serious discussion of risks, costs or benefits. Jobs, national security, economic security and the wellbeing of humans are all insignificant compared to the "environment."

In Tom Daschle's America, government knows best how to be charitable. Citizens are greedy and incapable of being compassionate enough to use their money and time to help the less fortunate in their communities.

In Tom Daschle's America, our soldiers should be sent to risk their lives, and possibly die, in the Middle East to keep the oil flowing, rather than drill on 2000 acres of barren and frozen tundra in Alaska.

In Tom Daschle's America, God, if he exists, should mind his own business when it comes to America. He was useful when he rallied the masses in 1776, but everything is under control now. He can move along. We don't need him now.

In Tom Daschle's America, only the federal government is qualified to make big decisions. State and local governments exist simply to collect the trash and arrest speeders.

In Tom Daschle's America, a free market cannot be trusted. Washington must manage health care, retirement investments, cable TV prices, software and computers and the water capacity of toilets.

In Tom Daschle's America, minorities can't possibly succeed without his help and the benefit of government sponsored racial preferences. How else can one fairly describe Tom's patronizing support of racial preferences?

In Tom Daschle's America, allowing Americans to take home more of their paycheck is a risky tax scheme and people who want to keep more of their own money are greedy and lack compassion.

Tom Daschle is leading his party and trying to lead this nation towards the America he envisions. He is intent on building a very different America and ignoring the Constitution. In his mind, the United States of America is like a ship that left port in 1776 and will finally reach her destination when we look like Europe.

Those of us who believe that America should reflect the ideals upon which it was founded have a moral obligation to stand against Tom Daschle and his followers. We should do so within the confines of that Constitution in which we so deeply believe, but we should stand firm.

Daschle and his allies know the greatest weakness of conservatives and of most Americans. We don't generally yell into bullhorns or stage protests in tree limbs. We don't chain ourselves to fences or stage sit-ins. We are too busy raising families, coaching little league teams, working to support ourselves and our families. Thus, it is easy to simply be a spectator as Tom Daschle steers America into dangerous waters. Daschle knows that a small rudder can redirect even the largest and grandest ship. Conservatives may be the engine, but Tom Daschle seeks to control the wheel.

Most of America is working in the bowels of the ship, stoking the furnace and greasing the machinery. If we are not careful, we will happily power this great ship to the European shores of neo-socialism. Americans cannot take their great heritage for granted. We must look out the window and see where the ship is headed and storm the wheelhouse.

Thoughts on Guns and Crime

(Originally published in August 2003)

Recently I toured a practice firing range for local police officers. The lead instructor and I talked at length about gun training, safety and technique. As the tour ended, our conversation turned to women and guns. I asked how many women actually carried guns. He answered, "Not enough." I was surprised. He pointed out that more women should to be trained and carry a concealed weapon, which is legal in my home state. He reasoned that those who are physically weaker gain the most benefit by protecting themselves.

The logic of the firearms instructor, although counter to the logic of our Million-Mom March culture, is consistent with the evidence of scholar John Lott who wrote *More Guns, Less Crime* and most recently, *The Bias Against Guns*. In his latest work, Lott turns the policies and arguments from the anti-gun crowd inside out to show that their "solutions" only perpetuate the problem. In *More Guns, Less Crime*, Lott presented research on defensive gun use vastly outweighs whatever benefits are alleged from gun control laws. In this follow-up book, *The Bias Against Guns,* Lott shows how anti-gun bias in the media taints and distorts the public's view of gun control laws.

Anti-gunners will definitely get hot under the collar at the conclusive research by Lott on defensive gun use. Facts are stubborn things and John Lott presents a wide array of stubborn facts to prove his point. From the bias in government research and media reporting, to the false premises underlying debates about gunlocks and whether pilots should be armed, Lott's book covers the hot button issues of the debate. Lott moves between anecdotal news and hard statistical evidence to uncover and prove the bias against guns.

Of course, most pro-gun Americans perceive a general loathing by the media. Most news stories and columnists seem to preach as truth that an armed public is a dangerous public. In analysis of news story after news story, Lott uncovers the reality of this bias. A memorable example was the reporting of a shooting in January of 2002 at a Virginia law school. A gunman opened fire on the campus and killed three students. He was stopped by three other students, two of whom had retrieved guns from their cars and were able to disarm the gunman and restrain him until the police arrived. During the week following the incident, over 200 news stories were written across the country. Of these, less than a hand-full even mentioned that the students were armed despite their heroics.

The bias, however, is not limited to those in media. Recently, federal, state and local governments have jumped on the bandwagon of gunlocks. Locks seem a viable solution to the headline news stories of accidental deaths among children because of a loaded and poorly stored weapon. In the last few years these stories, combined with school shootings, always seem to make national news. While the death of any individual is tragic, legislative and regulatory reactions should place facts over emotionally charged rhetoric. Center for Disease Control statistics from 1999 show more children die from bicycle accidents than from accidental gunfire. With the response we have seen to accidental gun deaths, it is surprising that more legislative work has not gone into bike safety, including helmets, training wheels and bike lane requirements for our communities by the Department of Transportation. Additionally, more children die in backyard pools each year than from accidental shootings. Perhaps we need more laws regulating pools and fences. The point is not to minimize any death, but to ask why some deaths are so publicized and so politicized and others, which happen with much greater frequency, are largely ignored. The answer reveals bias.

On the surface, safe storage laws imply any home will be safer. Why not encourage gun owners to have and use locks? Won't the home with a gun be safer if the gun has a trigger lock?

Lott observes that the most obvious problem with locks is that they make it extremely difficult to use a gun defensively. The best example of this is an incident with former Maryland Governor Parris Glendening. At a news conference to roll out his proposal for gunlocks, the Governor attempted to show how easy locks are to use. However, the demonstration backfired when he could not remove it. Finally several police officers had to step in and assist with the removal of the lock. With locks being this difficult to use, most people will quickly forego the lock. Moreover, if an attacker is on the scene, we can't reasonably count on his patience as we try to unlock the gun or on his assistance to get the gunlock off.

Those who swear by gun bans and waiting periods as well as card-carrying members of the National Rifle Association (NRA) will find Lott's work fascinating. Lott acknowledges that there are costs associated with having guns in society. However, there are also clear advantages that most fail to recognize. For example, in Great Britain, where there are strict gun control laws, nearly 60% of the burglaries occur when the residents are at home. Leaving citizens much more prone to being injured or killed while their home is burglarized. In contrast, in the United States were citizens are permitted to own guns, only 13% of burglaries occur when the resident is at home. Why? Because the incentive to "case a house" is much greater when a criminal considers that he might end up on the wrong side of a gun. Thus, American burglars tend to avoid a house that is occupied and British burglars don't seem to care who's home. As a result, far fewer Americans are killed or seriously harmed while their television is stolen. Simply stated, there are advantages to having guns in society—even if not everyone chooses to own one. It is high time we not only weigh the costs of having guns, but also begin to consider the advantages that gun ownership can bring to individuals and to our society.

John Lott takes a stand against the tide of popular opinion armed with stubborn facts. The most important of which is this—tighter gun restrictions not only hurt law-abiding citizens, but also perpetuate crime, adding to the problems they were supposed to solve.

Who's Telling the Truth on Judges?

(Originally published in November 2003)

Senate Republicans recently held more than thirty hours of straight debate to explain why President Bush's judicial nominees deserve a vote. They also hoped to force the Democrats to explain why they continue to block an unprecedented number of the president's judicial nominees.

Democrats decried this important substantive debate as a waste of time. However, only two days earlier the number two Democrat in the Senate, Harry Reid, clearly wasted nine hours of Senate debate time talking about sage brush and desert flowers and reading from a book he wrote about the small town of Searchlight, Nevada. After such a spectacle, how does one muster the audacity to accuse others of wasting time for scheduling a debate on the Senate's constitutionally mandated responsibility of "advice and consent" on judicial nominees?

But the real issue was whether it is appropriate for the Democrats to filibuster a number of the president's judicial nominees. Republicans argue that never before has the filibuster been used to block a slate of the judicial nominees to the federal circuit courts of appeal. This is true.

I teach constitutional law and one of the things I tell my students is that the first three rules of constitutional interpretation are (and the sequence of this is important): (1) read the document, (2) read the document, and (3) read the document. Senators Tom Daschle, Harry Reid, and Patrick Leahy and the rest of the obstructionists in the Senate would do well to enroll in my class.

They claim they are simply doing their job. But for the life of me, I can't find anything in the Constitution about postponing and delaying when it comes to the Senate's responsibility for confirming federal judges.

As I tell my students, let's read the document—the actual text of the Constitution. It is simple and direct. No great constitutional scholarship is required on this point. Article II, Section 2 says, "[The president] shall nominate, and by and with the advice and consent of the Senate, shall appoint…judges…" The Senate has a constitutional duty of "advice and consent," NOT postpone and delay.

But Democrats in the Senate are seeking to impose a super-majority requirement to confirm federal judges. Yet, this is contrary to the clear language and the intent of the Constitution.

In the same paragraph as the language that says that the Senate has the constitutional duty of advice and consent on federal judges, the Constitution does create a super-majority requirement for the ratification of treaties. Here is the actual language, "He shall have Power, by and with the Advice and Consent of the Senate, to make Treaties, provided two thirds of the Senators present concur..." So, it is clear that had the Founders intended a super-majority requirement, they could have imposed one—they did for treaties. But when it came to the confirmation of judges, the Founders specifically, clearly, and unambiguously rejected a super-majority requirement.

So, why do Senators like Daschle, Leahy and Reid, just to name a few, now seek to clandestinely amend the Constitution? Why do they seek to obstruct this important constitutional process? Why are they flouting the Constitution? The answer is simple—for partisan political gain!

Let me restate this point clearly because it is important—Senators Daschle, Leahy, Reid and most other Senate Democrats are, for their own partisan political purposes, disregarding their constitutional duties and flouting the Constitution.

Since they took an oath to uphold the Constitution, it is time for them to either resign in shame or do the job they took an oath to do and that is required by the Constitution!

These candidates are clearly qualified. Even the leftward leaning American Bar Association agrees. Senate Democrats said the ABA's stamp of approval was the "gold standard." But, apparently to a Senate Democrat even meeting or exceeding the "gold standard" is not good enough if President Bush nominated the judge.

This is about partisan politics—and it is unprecedented. Occasionally, uninformed folks will say things like, "Both parties do this" or "This is just the way things are done in Washington." That is simply false. The previous three presidents—Reagan, Bush and Clinton—had more than 90% of their circuit court nominees confirmed in less than one year. Moreover, an extended filibuster has *never* been used to block the nomination of a federal appeals court judge.

Messrs. Daschle, Leahy and Reid and many Senate Democrats, you have taken an oath of office. By any reasonable standard you have violated that oath. Instead of permitting the constitutional process of nominating and confirming judges to move forward, you have played partisan politics from the first day this president took office—almost three years ago. It is one thing to play politics with political matters, but it is entirely another to do it with a solemn constitutional duty.

The time is past due. Allow the Senate to vote. Allow the Senate to fulfill its constitutional mandate. If the nominees are unacceptable to the full Senate, so be it. But stop the partisan postponing, delaying and obstructing. And stop the lying about what you doing and why.

When will you find time to live up to your oath of office? When will you find time to uphold the Constitution as you've sworn to do? If not now, when?

Rogue Judges and the Constitution

(Originally published in January 2004)

Too many judges can no longer be counted on to reach rational and reasonable decisions based on the law. Instead, too many judges now regularly issue decisions based on the absurd and the fanciful. To make matters worse, these same judges impose their political views on the rest of us through anti-democratic and politically unaccountable means and then they tell us the Constitution made them do it. Understandably, much of the public is beginning to view these judges as freak-show entertainers rather than dispassionate arbiters of the law. We are all the poorer for it. Here are just three recent examples.

First, earlier this year, the U.S. Supreme Court in a 5-to-4 vote rejected the plain language of the First Amendment and held that the government can regulate and even ban some forms of political speech within sixty days of an election when it upheld the unconstitutional campaign finance bill.

The First Amendment clearly states, "Congress shall make no law...abridging the freedom of speech." This unequivocal language has, in the past, been broadly used by the Court to protect flag burning and pornography—even forms of child pornography. But somehow, the Court could not find the language clear enough or broad enough to protect legitimate political speech shortly before an election—the very time such political discourse is most needed.

One must be an intellectual contortionist to make sense of the Court's rulings. Simply stated, that which the Constitution clearly and unequivocally requires—the right of free speech—the Court simply ignores and in so doing turns the Constitution on its head.

Second, the highest court in Massachusetts ruled that homosexual marriage is a fundamental constitutional right. The court then completely outdid itself and ordered the Massachusetts legislature to pass "appropriate" legislation within 180 days. In so doing, the court usurped the role of legislator and abandoned its role of arbiter of the law. So much for separation of powers. The court in Massachusetts apparently believes the legislature works for the court and answers to the court.

Folks are free to argue that the law should permit homosexual marriages. Likewise, I am free to argue that marriage is and must remain the legal union of one man and one woman. This is a fair debate that ultimately is decided by the people through their elected representatives. But it is simply indefensible and laugh-

206 On Politics and Policy

able to argue that the people have no say in the matter and that the Constitution mandates the approval of homosexual marriage. Yet, this is precisely what the court did.

The proper role of the courts is to adjudicate legitimate legal disputes. The role of the legislature is to make laws. The courts have forgotten this separation of powers, taken off their judicial robes and overthrown the will of the people as expressed by the legislators they elected. This is the behavior of a dictator or a despot. John Adams, the second President of the United States and the original author of Massachusetts' constitution, would be shocked and appalled.

Third, last year the Ninth Circuit Court of Appeals ruled that the words "under God" in the Pledge of Alliance are an unconstitutional establishment of religion—even though the Constitution does not forbid the mention of God in public. The Constitution provides a wise balance—a prohibition against state established religion and the freedom to worship according to the dictates of our conscience. Yet, some courts completely ignore the Free Exercise Clause because of their hostility to religion. Judges, who ignore one half of the equation, are bound to get the wrong answer.

I teach constitutional law and always tell my students on the first day of class that there are three fundamental rules of constitutional interpretation. These rules are: first, read the document; second, read the document; and third, read the document. The U.S. Supreme Court, the Massachusetts high court, and the Ninth Circuit Court of Appeals would do well to enroll in my class.

It is interesting that this attack on America's Constitution and its democratic institutions is lead not simply by rogue judges, but also in large part by the American Civil Liberties Union (ACLU). Together rogue judges and the ACLU act as a battering ram to dismantle the Constitution. What makes their destructive actions all the more outrageous is that they claim to be preserving the Constitution as they work to dismantle it.

Words have meanings and so do constitutions. Courts simply do not have the right to ignore the clear meaning of the Constitution and impose their personal political views on society. Judges who do this violate their sworn oath of office and ought to step down. If judges prefer to legislate, they should take off their judicial robes and run for Congress. There they can legislate to their heart's content. But to legislate from the bench as an unelected and unaccountable judge diminishes our representative democracy and weakens the Constitution.

There are plenty of other examples of courts run amok. Courts have tried to force the Boy Scouts to drop a duty to God from the Scout Oath and allow homosexual scout leaders. There is no shortage of examples. But the question is what to do about it. Some suggest that we need constitutional amendments—redefining political speech, defining marriage, banning flag burning, protecting the Boy Scouts—just to name a few.

There certainly is a problem, but it is not the Constitution. It is irresponsible judges. Despite what some rogue judges may say, the Constitution does not grant government the power to regulate political speech before elections, or require recognition of gay marriage or remove words from the Pledge of Alliance.

If irresponsible, rogue judges are the problem—and they certainly are—why should we be forced to mount an effort to amend the Constitution—a very difficult process—just to undo the rogue judges' outlandish and illegal deeds? What guarantees do we have that these same judges won't simply ignore and flout the newest amendments to the Constitution?

I do not oppose well-written constitutional amendments that undo the damage of rogue judges and return our jurisprudence to its original meaning before it was polluted by activist judges. We must prevent those who mean to overthrow our form of government from doing so. But I am nervous that the same rogue judges who disregarded the Constitution in the first place will simply disregard the amendments. These rogue judges violate their oath of office, lay siege to the Constitution and our laws and demean our representative democracy.

This means that judges must be selected carefully. It also means that Americans must demand that rogue judges—those who refuse to uphold their oath of office and instead act as unelected, unaccountable legislators—be removed from office. It should not be controversial to expect judges to uphold their oath of office and respect the Constitution.

If we don't wake up soon, we will have lost the greatest system for self-government known to man. What is happening is the slow and gradual overthrow of the Constitution by judges who have sworn to uphold and defend it. At some point, Americans must stand up and demand that judges uphold the Constitution rather than undermine it.

George Washington and his army of patriots fought against all odds to free Americans from the oppression of an unelected, life-tenured king and an out-of-control parliament. They did not make these sacrifices so that 225 years later a group of life-tenured and out-of-control judges could crown themselves our despotic rulers.

Ronald Reagan: Where Does He Rank?

(Originally published in June 2004)

With the passing of former President Ronald Wilson Reagan, numerous political analysts from all sides of the political spectrum have opined that Reagan was indisputably one of the greatest presidents of the Twentieth Century. I have no problem with that assessment. But it raises an interesting question. If we were to list the greatest presidents ever, who would be placed ahead of Ronald Reagan? Not many.

Presidential greatness is determined by making an enduring positive impact—by changing the course of history for the better. By this standard, few are Ronald Reagan's equal. He changed the way Americans viewed themselves and the way the world viewed America. America had endured more than two decades of embarrassments and a downward spiral. Most believed that America was a nation in decline. Conventional wisdom was that communism might be contained, but never defeated. Most intellectuals believed that the United States would eventually lose the Cold War and that communism was the wave of the future.

Ronald Reagan believed none of this. He believed America's best days lay ahead. He believed in the innate goodness of America and Americans. He had an undying confidence and trust that America, freedom and right would prevail. Some thought him naïve and even simple. They were wrong. Ronald Reagan was right.

Ronald Reagan's leadership led to an economic revival in America that continues to this day. Reagan made Americans proud again and he taught America that we could believe in ourselves. His leadership protected the United States and the world from violent and ruthless totalitarianism. Reagan's leadership led to the defeat of communism when only a few years earlier, the Soviet Union was viewed as overtaking America in military, economic and political might. Ronald Reagan's leadership changed the terms of debate. He strengthened and renewed America. He gave hope and freedom to hundreds of millions around the world.

What other presidents can match that record?

George Washington, the Father of our nation, is our greatest president. He is perhaps the one man who was indispensable to American independence and the difficult task of establishing a stable democracy. He is the man for whom the office of president was written. He led the colonies to defeat the greatest military power then known to man. He presided over the creation of our famed Constitution. He carefully created the precedents that made our president respected by foreign powers, but kept the Presidency from becoming royalty. He set the highest standards for integrity and honesty in public service and he willingly walked away from power, setting the precedent that political power is not a lifetime gift.

Once you get past George Washington, what other presidents could be placed higher on the list than Reagan? Not many. Here are a few names that are commonly listed as among our best presidents—Thomas Jefferson, Abraham Lincoln, Teddy Roosevelt and Franklin Roosevelt. Each faced many challenges and each exerted remarkable leadership. But none of these, as president and without the aid of armed conflict, made the sort of dramatic change to America and to the world that Ronald Reagan did.

Ronald Reagan stands alone as a visionary leader who, by the sheer power of his ideas and the quality of his leadership, changed America and the world and made both safer, freer and more prosperous.

My point is not to criticize or detract from other presidents. America has been blessed with many great patriots and leaders. But it is clear that it is not enough to recognize Ronald Reagan as one of the greatest presidents of the Twentieth Century. Ronald Reagan is one of our greatest presidents—period—of any century, of any time.

It is said that a nation can be judged by the heroes it honors. No nation has been more blessed than America with great and worthy heroes. Our founding alone provides George Washington, John Adams, Benjamin Franklin, and Thomas Jefferson—*to name only a few*. In modern times, none stands taller than Ronald Reagan. I am proud for America to be judged by numbering Ronald Reagan as one of our chief heroes.

0-595-33571-3

www.ingramcontent.com/pod-product-compliance
Lightning Source LLC
Chambersburg PA
CBHW061400280526
45784CB00001B/324